Once Upon a Pony

by Vicki Austin

This book is dedicated to my grandchildren for
they have all taken a part in riding.
Some ride just to please me.
Some ride every chance they get. All love Baby.

ISBN: 978-1-4269-9391-6 (sc)
ISBN: 978-1-4269-9392-3 (e)

Trafford rev. 08/27/2011

 PUBLISHING® www.trafford.com

North America & international
toll-free: 1 888 232 4444 (USA & Canada)
phone: 250 383 6864 ♦ fax: 812 355 4082

Acknowledgments

I want to thank my husband of 41 years who has been after me for the last ten years to write a book about my teaching and training experiences. He has been there for me my whole adult life. He somehow understands the pull that horses have for me, especially Baby.

I want to extend a huge thank you to my daughter in law Abigail Austin. She is my editor and helped me through this writing experience. She started out as a student and became a friend whom I love. We have shared many fun times. Without her expertise, this book would be just a jumble of words.

I want to thank Pat and Cassie Martin (Pat's daughter) of Painted Pony Sport Horses and Equestrian Center for taking such good care of Baby. They continue to humor me with my many wants and wishes and to pamper Baby. I also want to thank Cassie for the wonderful lessons she gives Baby and I so that we keep flexible and balanced in our old ages, and for keeping Baby exercised while I am out of town.

I thank my dear friend Suzanne Thorndike. Without the gift of Baby, I would have no story to tell. As a team, we raised Baby. We shared many lunches of tuna fish and onion sandwiches and sugar free hot chocolate. This only Sue and I will remember for we shared these with no one. I have really missed Sue since she moved south but have shared Baby's accomplishments with her, as we call each other to catch up on our lives often.

"EASY BOOT BRIDGE" was published in an earlier version in Chicken Soup for the Horse Lover's Soul II, Health Communications,Inc, Deerfield Beach, Florida, 2006

Some names have been changed to maintain privacy.

baby

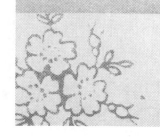

BABY, BABY

She arrived in the middle of a warm night while all was quiet except for the sigh of a soft breeze and the new spring peepers.

When I came into the barn, a soft nicker greeted me from the stall in the back left corner. It was a large stall, made for foaling, with deep bedded straw just waiting for the new baby that was soon to arrive. I said, "Good morning Bonny. Hungry?" As I looked over the four foot door and into Bonny's stall the cutest grayish-brown face with tiny ears peeked out from around Bonny's legs. It wasn't evident if it was a filly or colt, but it just stood and looked at me with huge doe eyes and the wonder of all new born babies.

"Oh my goodness, Bonny, what have we here?" I asked Bonny, who was a twelve hand pony I was training for a dear friend of mine. "I was hoping to be here when you foaled, you sneaky little pony!"

Bonny's owner, Suzanne Thorndike, had brought her to me a few months prior for training. It seemed that she was overweight, and I exercised her to slim her down. Then I saw movement in her belly. A visit from the vet confirmed my suspicions.

Bonny nickered to me again more urgently "Enough with the small talk" she seemed to be saying, "Yeah she's cute, now please feed me!"

I woke from my daydream, "Sorry, Bonny, just a minute." I opened Bonny's stall door and walked in to check over her new little treasure. "Hi, little one. Aren't you just the cutest little thing?" I said as I walked up to pet the tiny foal, which I could see now was a filly . She started walking towards me and...

The little bugger bit me! Then she turned around, squealed and kicked me!

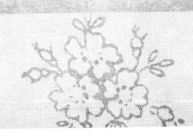

The surprise of it left me speechless for a moment. I just couldn't believe how much power that tiny filly had. Horses are born without teeth for nursing and soft hooves that wouldn't hurt the mother during gestation. I guessed she didn't like having her space invaded. After the shock of it all ,I couldn't help but laugh right out loud. " You are one tough little baby aren't you?"

After feeding the horses, I phoned Bonny's owner, Suzanne, to share the news. Within ten minutes, while I was photographing the foal, Sue was by my side.

"Oh Vicki, she is so cute!" Sue exclaimed, "So tiny and just perfect."

Sue was looking at Bonny and her new baby. "But what am I going to do with her?" She looked thoughtful for a moment. "I think it only fitting that she stay here with you since she was born here."

I tried to hide my shock as I certainly didn't need or *want* a foal to raise. I had my hands full with my riding school, twelve horses, and ponies working least eight hours a day with lessons. Plus I had two horses in for training. I didn't have time to raise a foal.

While my husband, Ron, and I raised three teenage boys,I was trying to run a successful riding. I kept twelve horses and ponies, worked eight hours a day teaching lessons, plus I had horses in for training. Ron was very supportive of my dream to help young riders on their way and often worked overtime to help with the costs of running a business and raising a family. I didn't have time to raise a foal.

I did not want to hurt Suzanne's feelings as she saw keeping the foal as a gift, so I simply thanked her without much enthusiasm. "She is awfully cute, maybe we could sell her when weaned or make her into a good driving pony or lesson pony." I figured.

"Maybe. Won't get much without papers but we will see" she replied. We both had had our share of "raising babies" both human and horse.

I looked into the stall "Well, we better get some iodine on her umbilical cord to ward of infection. And just check to make sure everything looks OK. Would you like to help me?" I asked as I walked over to get the iodine from the medicine cabinet that I kept in the barn and set it just outside the stall door.

"She is a bit of a witch about her space" I said with a snicker.

Sue looked at me kind of suspiciously. "Isn't she a little young to be witchy about anything?"

"Watch." I walked in the stall. I was not surprised this time as the filly once again walked over and bit me. She turned around to kick, almost falling down in her haste. "See?" I just couldn't help but laugh, it was just too funny!

"Wow! She is bad! I never would have believed it!" Sue exclaimed.

I went to the foal's side and wrapped my arms around her neck. She struggled to try to get away. I had her backed into the corner. "Not so fast little one. I am a little bigger than you are at the moment." I said with a little chuckle.

Bonny nickered.

"Don't worry mama, I won't hurt her," I said to her.

"Here, Sue, do you want to check her over? I will have you hold her while I put the iodine on afterwards."

Sue looked at me, looked at the filly. "OK, sure." Sue looked her over and pronounced her perfectly normal as far as we could see.

"Put your arms around her like I am."

She did, and the filly ceased to struggle as she saw no escape. But her ears were as flat against her head as was possible, her lips in a sneer, eyes murderous. If looks could kill! I got the iodine and dabbed where the umbilical cord had been. Then while Sue had a hold of her I touched her all over, imprinting the foal, which introduced her to human contact on her entire body.

After we were done, we left the stall and leaned on the door as we chatted about her unusual color. The foal laid down and immediately feel asleep, while Bonny contentedly munched hay.

We couldn't help but notice Appaloosa markings, none of which Bonny had. The little one had tiny spots around her muzzle and eyes, (eyes that followed me any time I was within sight), striped hooves, and party-colored around her udder and beneath her tail. Her coat, being dusty gray, looked like it would be bay (dark brown). Her mane and tail were black with little bits of tan baby fuzz in it.

We had no idea who her dad was. Was he a horse or a pony? Pony of Americas (POA) perhaps? But there hadn't been any at the dealers.

Suzanne purchased Bonny from a horse dealer, which is an organization or person who buys and sells horses and ponies for profit. As with the case with Bonny a buyer may never know where the horse comes from, or even its age or breed. What you see is what you get.

There had been, however, one recently gelded Appaloosa colored horse at that dealer. Geldings can father a foal up to a month after being gelded. Even though the dealer *said* the mare had not been out with a stallion and could not be in foal, breeding could still have occurred with a recently gelded horse. Surprise! Here is this tiny foal.

She certainly was a different kind of foal with an attitude. I kept looking at her. *Nope, don't need another pony. Don't want another pony. Don't have time for a foal.* Still, she tugged at my heart, especially with her strong personality. I saw a challenge ahead for whoever ended up with her.

For a couple of days, Sue and I threw around some names for the foal and considered her apparent Appaloosa heritage with American Indians.

It was during one of our famous lunches that we named Baby.

"How about Indy?" Sue suggested.

"But she has to have a fancy name as well," I replied, with my mouthful of tuna.

"Well, let's see." Sue was cocking her head to the side in deep thought. She took a drink of coco. "Indian something with Indy for short. Hmmm. There are a lot of signs that she has Appy in her lineage--how about Indian Sign? Indian Smoke? Indian Signal? Smoky Indian? Smoke Signal?"

I was in deep thought as I paused my eating, mind reeling with her suggestions. "I know!" It suddenly came to me. "Indian Smoke Sign with Indy for short !" I said excitedly.

"Oh, I like that!" said Sue.

Thus we agreed on her name. We found ourselves simply calling her "The Baby" and later on just Baby. "Witchy Woman" would have suited her better because that is what I ended up calling her most of the time,

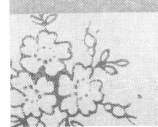
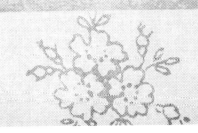

even singing part of the song, "OOOO HOOO Witchy Woman." She was a very crabby pony. I also found myself calling her "Big Butt Baby" or "Piggy Baby" because she had a tendency to want to eat all the time.

At a week old, I put Bonny and Baby out in the pasture. At first Baby just stayed by her mom and either slept or nursed. Before long, she was the terrorist in the herd. It puzzled me that she never was very afraid of the other horses. She would walk up to them, not even giving the submission sign, the silent gum chewing action that all foals give when meeting an older horse. Then she would strike with lightning speed, and either bite a nose, rear up and strike or turn, squeal and kick whatever she could reach. Then she would hightail it back to her mom and hide behind her. Bonny would shake her head at the other horses if they dared to come near. Don't mess with a new mother!

After about three weeks, when Baby would start for another horse, they would try to attack her. Somehow she was almost always faster and quicker and got away without a scratch. But once in a while, one of them would catch her unawares and get her back a good one.

Silver (Arab, pony cross) would chase her around and bite her butt. Boy (big chestnut Quarter Horse) would stand his ground and click his teeth, but pretty much just ignore her. Since he was no fun, Baby would venture over to Dusty (Appaloosa Thoroughbred cross) and he would start for her before she got there. Zokeema (Arabian, pony cross we bought from Sue) tried to get Baby to play with her because she thought Baby was playing a game by chasing her, so she did the same. Old Pat (pinto Shetland in his 30s) did his best to stay out of Baby's way and would hide in the barn shadows. Lou Lou (beautiful Bay Standardbred) would start swinging her head any time Baby came near, and blow raspberries at her. Jodee (POA) followed Baby

around, trying to tell her what she could and could not do, of course to no avail. It wasn't long before none of the others really liked her at all. She was running out of potential friends fast.

In came "Old Grandpa" Colonel, a retired, true black, Standardbred that the other horses respected. He'd been watching her antics from afar. Baby finally ventured to Colonel.

Before Baby could strike, he took hold of her with his teeth by her crest, the top of her neck where it is fatty. He picked her up, shook her, and then put her down.

Baby froze. She looked at him, not quite believing that she wasn't the princess that she thought she was. This horse was different. She cocked her head to the side and gave the submission sign to him.

Colonel nodded his head up and down then nuzzled her. They had a conversation that only they knew the meaning.

Then she slowly walked back to her mom and I could see her thinking, as she kept looking back at him. She laid down for a nap in Bonny's pile of hay, and was passive the rest of the day, leaving everyone alone.

When Bonny tired of protecting her from the other horses, Baby turned to Colonel who became her savior. She stood behind him, as far under his tail as she could get, with her nose poking out.

With his tail over her face, all I could see were her large doe eyes and her tiny ears in amongst his heavy long tail. It looked like a rockers long locks, gone wild. Colonel kept an eye on Baby like a body guard, stepping in when he saw another horse start to retaliate against her. Without even a bite or kick he would stomp his foot to command "Ten Hut!" and they all seemed to know what he meant.

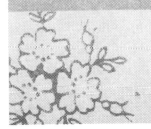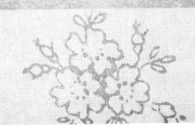

Baby got away with terrorizing the others and became a very bad pony, bullying them especially if she wanted their pile of hay. If they lifted a hoof or barred teeth, she was very quick to run to hide behind "Grandpa Colonel." She knew there would be no pay back with him there. She was a very smart, little devil.

Eventually even Bonny was her target. She would walk up to Bonny to nurse, but when Bonny walked away, she would bite and kick her. Bonny would stop, sigh and resign herself to this abuse, but was showing signs of wear and getting thin even though she was eating a *lot* of food.

I secretly loved Baby's spunk and couldn't wait to start working with her so I decided to give the herd a break and Baby a job very early in life.

Four weeks old with vicki.

Baby was just four weeks old when I took her for her first walk. She had been wearing a little goat halter since she was only a day old and had been handled and led behind her mom ever since.

I decided it was time to take her away from the others, including her mom, who needed the break more than anyone. I put the lead on Baby and started to lead her out through the gate.

Baby realized that this was different. She wasn't following Mom this time. She suddenly put on the brakes at the gate, legs bracing, neck stretched out as far as it could go, ears flat back, eyes wild and evil looking.

"Oh no you don't!" I said as I dragged her through the gate.

Up she went! Baby reared straight up almost as erect as a person, and struck my shoulder with a front hoof. When she came down, she bit me on the leg.

No sooner had I recovered and taken firmer hold, she swung and kicked me! WOW ! The speed and power in that little demon was amazing!

I was able to quickly close the gate and get her to move forward in this fashion, with me pulling, her bracing and then attacking. Although the walk was only about fifteen minutes long, it was long enough as I tried to hold on to this tiny tornado.

She only weighed in at about eighty pounds, but that was the strongest eighty pounds I had ever had the dismay to handle. I had all I could do to hang on to her, and I put her back in the pasture very quickly. When I let her go, she took one more kick at me as she galloped away. I had to think about this for a day or two. I wasn't about to let her get the best of me.

The next time I took Baby for a walk, I used a chain over her nose. When she reared and struck me with her hooves, I snapped the lead, shouting, "No!" I did it again when she spun to kick, spinning her body

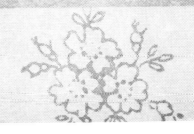

around. It worked. To this day she reacts to the word "no." In over twenty-one years (and now over forty years) that was the only time I had to do that to a foal, but she was a terror. It would be her or me. Baby's lesson was just that long, but her learning was profound. She is very smart.

Baby was rotund by the time she was three months old however Bonny's condition had deteriorated to the point that her weight was not healthy despite the feed she consumed.

I felt it time to wean Baby. Typically I didn't wean foals until six or eight months if they still needed to nurse and their moms were happy. However Baby was eating hay and grain with no problem. She didn't need her mother's milk.

I walked Bonny down to Sue's house nearby, and left Baby behind. Bonny seemed relieved, even heaving a sigh. Baby didn't really care. She just kept on eating but watched me out of the corner of her eye. Always watching. Neither pony even whinnied. It was as if "good riddance" was the order of the day. There never was any separation anxiety at all. Another new experience for me!

That evening, Baby came in with the rest of the horses, went into the stall that up till now she had shared with her mother. Now it was her stall, and she settled right in without a peep.

POOR BABY!

Porka

Since I had given my own vaccines for over twenty years, I planned on giving Baby hers when she was

weaned. Even though it was early, she was no longer protected by Mama's milk.

I put Baby on the cross ties, leads that hung from opposite sides of the wall that hooked to her halter. I gave her a small handful of grain, which she always loved. I swabbed alcohol in the nice little triangle of space in her neck.

This triangle is visible on the necks of all horses. The center is the best place to give an intramuscular vaccine. This would not be near any vital bones, and not too far into the fatty crest which would slow its absorption.

Baby snorted at the smell and cool feel of the alcohol. "Isn't that a funny smell, Baby?" I asked. She soon accepted it.

I pinched the skin where I had swabbed the alcohol and inserted the needle. She jumped a little. "Ops, Baby, you are OK. I promise you are."

Baby stood with a puzzled look in her eye. She, of course, was looking right at my face. I gave her another small bit of grain. "Good girl!"

I tapped and squirted the syringe to get all air bubbles out, then attached it to the needle in Baby's neck. She wiggled a little, about what I expected.

"OK, little girl. Your first baby shot." I plunged in the solution. I was *not* prepared for the reaction she was to have!

She made the most horrible scream! I quickly pulled out the needle and syringe. But it was too late.

I felt Baby's wrath as she bit at me, missing my arm only by inches as I jumped back in surprise!

Baby reared up on the cross ties and flipped over backwards. She hung upside down with her back on the floor and her head still up in the cross ties, legs flailing. I quickly released the emergency tie on one side

and let her right herself. I started shaking, my heart pounding, wondering what horrible thing I had done to her!

"Holy crap, you must be very sensitive, Baby" I panted. "Oh, my God, what did I just do?!"

I continued to shake, my legs feeling like jelly , wondering if I had hit a vital organ or something. "I am so sorry, Baby!" I exclaimed. "I know it was in the correct spot. I just *know* it. I couldn't have hurt *that* much."

I gave a minute for me to settle a bit. My heart was still pounding as I was wondering what to do next. She made eye contact with hurt eyes. I had betrayed her. I had hurt her!

My heart was breaking and tears began to form as I wanted to cry! *Nope! Be tough. All you did was give shots.* I told myself. I had done this many many times with many many horses.

"There, Baby, are you OK now?" I checked the site and saw nothing amiss. I felt confident that all was as it should be. I offered her grain. Baby accepted. I was forgiven. I then hugged her. "I am so sorry Baby! Sorry that it hurt."

I was dismayed that by the end of the day Baby could not put her head down to eat. This kind of thing had never happened before in over twenty years of giving my own vaccinations.

I called my vet, who said to give her some bute (horse aspirin) for the next couple of days. He told me that it does happen in a few sensitive horses every year.

That didn't make me feel any better about it.

I put up a hay bag for her so she could eat, and for the first time gave her a bute for her pain. I broke it up into quarters and put it into chunks of apple. Since she thought of it as a "treat", she took it right out of my hand, and ate it, looking for more. It took three days before she could lower her head to eat normally.

I died a thousand deaths, I felt so crummy that I had hurt her.

To this day, twenty two years later, Baby still fights me on the vaccinations if she sees it coming. The vet usually has me give the rabies because she is just so horrible. I have learned to surprise her and have it done before she knows what is happening. Giving shots in the traditional way meant either being bitten, kicked or struck. Using a twitch only made it worse as she went wild, and what would be the point of a tranquilizer *shot* to give her regular vaccines?

Receiving vaccinations left her very swollen at the needle site for days no matter how carefully the shot was administered. She always would, and it never failed, be sore to the point of not being able to lower her head to eat.

To combat this, I had the idea to give her bute two feedings before and two feedings after her shots to lesson the pain, but never could lesson her... fear?...hate?...indignity?

I had to think of nontraditional ways to do this. I had to protect her against disease. Discomfort was the lesser of the two evils. Some horse diseases will kill while shots will just be inconvenient for a while.

Now the scenario goes like this. I will meditate beforehand to keep me calm. Then as in routine grooming, I take my fists either bare or in a towel as if strapping a muscle in good shape. She never knows when I will in one quick motion give her a shot. I just aim, jab and squirt all in one quick smooth motion.

She jumps out of her half-masted sleepy-eyed "I love being groomed" mode, and then I continue the pounding or strapping motion as if nothing happened.

I keep my poker face, although my heart is beating fast and I am dying inside having to do this.

I give her a quick message of the area and a treat to distract her more. I continue her grooming, tack her up and go for a short ride to try to help the vaccine absorb better. By excising a horse, it gets the blood moving and helps the vaccines to absorb better and quicker.

How can it be that to protect a horse from some horribly nasty conditions and diseases, you have to hurt them. They do not understand this. I don't either.

HOW SMART CAN A PONY BE?

Coming home from worship services to find your foal loose and running fence trying to get back in is *not* how you want to start your Sunday afternoon.

I got out of the car in my dress and heels and proceeded to go "catch" Baby. "Come here. How in the world did you get out?"

She ran over to me, nickering and shoving/nudging her nose into my stomach. There was never any need for "catching" as she saw every opportunity for a hand out. She came to me, and I gave her the ever present snack, this time a handful of green grass growing around my heels. It was good enough for her. I wrapped my arm around her neck and guided her in through the gate that I had opened with my other hand. I pondered how strange it is that horses can manage to get out but never figure out how to get back in!

Later after lunch and changing my clothes, I walked the fence, puzzled as to how she managed to get out. Nothing was out of place and everything was peaceful. With post and rail and three strands of electric inside it, the last strand only eighteen inches from the ground, It was unlikely that anyone could escape. Somehow Baby had, and there was no way she jumped the five foot post and rail with the added three or so inches that electric on top was! It just wasn't physically possible. With her mother gone from the farm, Baby found all kinds of things to amuse herself. She managed to "get out" regularly so I decided to leave a halter on her in case a stranger had to "catch" her as she wasn't so easy to catch if she didn't know you.

"OK Baby, now how did you manage that?" This time I came home to find her standing up against the fence looking so very sad. She whinnied to me the moment she saw me.

"What the heck?" I ran down to the fence saw that somehow she had her halter ring caught in the electric fence insulator and was just standing there waiting to be rescued. Why she wasn't getting zapped is beyond me. She could easily have freaked out and pulled the whole fence down but instead she felt she was "tied"! Probably because she had spent so much time tied, that she felt she should stay "tied."

I ran into the barn and turned off the fencer. I wasn't going to get zapped rescuing her.

Baby whinnied the whole time I was gone out of her sight, in her shrill voice (which she still has today at age twenty-two). "Don't leave me!" she seemed to be saying.

"OK Baby, I am coming! Wait one minute." I unhooked her halter to set her free. She stood right there watching me as I spent a few minutes untangling her little halter from the insulator. When I had it free, she walked over and put her head back in the halter and nuzzled me. Then she spun around and ran off to see Colonel. I looked at the fence, still puzzled over that trick.

"Oh my goodness! Honey, come and see this" I was doing the dinner dishes and looking out the window at the pasture and the horses. My husband, Ron, knew it was probably something to do with the horses so he took his time, grabbing his coffee and came to look at what had caught my attention.

"I just can't believe it!" I said.

"Well, I guess she is smart, huh?" He replied.

There was Baby, shoulder to the ground, neck stretched out sideways, with the side of her head flat against the ground. Her front legs were off to the side. Her butt was up in the air, and her tail swatted back and forth. Baby's lips were working fast to get every single morsel of green grass within reach *under* the bottom strand of electric fence.

I watched in awe! She sure was limber.

She plopped her butt down. Now all four legs were on one side and she was flat on the ground. In a shimmying motion, she managed to get herself under the fence, all except her big butt, which just barely touched the electric fence. She jumped up in the air like a cat that had been startled, and ran for her life.

Ron almost spewed his coffee as we both started laughing, witnessing her escape.

In between bursts of giggles, I managed to say ,"I guess I better go get her."

I lamented, "What am I going to do with her if we cannot keep her fenced?"

"Well, we could get rid of her. Then you won't have to worry about it." That was his answer anytime I complained about the horses. Although I knew he was fooling, it still made me a little angry.

By the time I had gone out, Baby had decided that it had been worth it to get zapped and was happily eating the treasured green grass that she'd wanted so badly.

"Baby, come here girl," I called her. She walked over to me, happy to go in the barn where her grain awaited.

BACK AND FORTH

"Sue, would you like to have Baby live down there for a while?" A few weeks later I called Sue.

By now Baby was about a year old, and I had had about enough of her antics. I had exhausted all my ideas for keeping her in the pasture. I needed a break, and she just needed to grow up a little. I also needed to replace our fencing. The other horses respected temporary electric fencing. For Baby, it just meant a minor obstacle to simply scoot under or reach through. Getting zapped would only make her hurry, possibly breaking the tape fencing and letting all the others out with her. This could be disastrous because I lived on a well-traveled road.   Sue had a more secure paddock. It was fenced with page wire five feet high. It had electric wire on the inside so that the ponies wouldn't press on it and escape. I was hoping it would be a perfect system to keep in Baby.

Sue replied, "Sure, I will keep her."

We agreed that I would continue to work with Baby. I'd keep the other two larger ponies in shape for Sue in exchange for Baby's care. Whether I had her or Sue had her, Baby would need handling. It would be a job for two "mamas." This was easy to do since Sue was my neighbor, and being retired had plenty of time to play with Baby.

Sue gave me a knowing look. "If she causes trouble, though, you get her right back." she said half joking.

Baby did cause trouble, but Sue, thought she was very entertaining to watch.

She chased little Stacy (bay Shetland pony) around immediately. She tried to chase Zodee (Arab pony cross, and Zokeema's mom) but got put in her place with a swift kick to her chest. Bonny, Baby's mother, could not be bothered with her at all, just gave a nasty look with a swing of her head and barred teeth. Baby left her alone.

Baby seemed very happy at Sue's and lived at night in a stand stall alongside the other ponies. They ate side by side and could see each other and talk to each other. The stalls were about four feet wide, and had rubber mats, so there was plenty of room to lie down comfortably. Each pony had a full hay bag at night. Baby felt grown up and within the first week showed a little sign of maturity she had yet to show at my barn.

Stacy finally stopped running from Baby, so Baby left her alone. Zodee established that she was the boss of the place. It is hard to chase when no one runs. Baby stopped trying.

TIME FOR SCHOOL

Baby sucked in her breath each time the saddle blanket made contact, quivering as I put it up against her body and back and pulled it away again.

"Come on, Baby, this is soft and cuddly," I said as she wiggled and jiggled, trying to get away. She was frightened of the blanket I fluttered about her head and body. Getting horses used to blankets to wear, saddle blankets, pads and other items of horse wear is important. Not only will they have to eventually wear them, they need to feel comfortable that nothing humans have in their hands is going to harm them. She finally realized that the blanket wasn't going to eat her, but kept a wary eye on it.

"That's better. See? Not so bad, you silly little girl," I gave her a generous handful of grain as a goody to tell her how proud of her I was. She lowered her head.

"OK now, this one is going to be tougher, Baby girl," I said as I then got out the bag of empty, plastic milk bottles and brushed it over her body.

These not only felt funny they made noise! Once again, Baby jigged back and forth on the cross ties. She tried to rear. She kicked out behind. She stomped her front feet. She was wild eyed.

"Baby it's OK. You need to know that these things will not hurt you."

I kept on *torturing* her in this way until she once again she resigned herself to my will. "What a good girl," I praised and petted her. Little by little as I repeated these lessons, she began to ignore the strange stuff. Baby lowered her head and gave a gentle chewing sign of submission. More goodies.

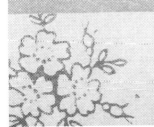

I spent countless hours "sacking her out" in this fashion. Day after day I put blankets, pads, saddles, bridles, grain bags, and anything else I could think of on top, underneath and around her. I led her over tarps, poles on the ground, and over bridges in the preserve. I even covered her head with towels, and led her around that way so she would completely trust me.

Sue and I put hanging plastic milk jugs with water or pebbles in her stall for her to play with so she would not get bored. It also helps to get used to the sounds that the contents made moving around in the jugs.

I put a huge hard plastic "horse ball" in the pasture for her to roll around, with a bell inside for all the horses to play with, that would not fit under the fence and roll away..

Taking all that time now while Baby was still young was the best way to get her used to just about anything and make her a safe confident mount. Since Baby was two weeks old, I'd handled her in order to get her accustomed to various handling in the future. I picked up her feet and cleaned them daily, even rasping them, which would be similar to how a farrier would work with her to trip her hooves and set shoes. I put my fingers in her mouth so she would accept dental work, oral medicine, like de-wormer and a bit.

Of all Baby's handling, her favorite part was the grooming. The downside to her sensitivity was her reaction to her vaccinations, but the positive side was how good it felt to her to be groomed. She especially loved having her ears handled, messaged, and brushed, and would nicker her appreciation.

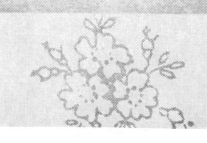

Two year old Baby living at Sue's

I started lunging Baby at two years old for just a few minutes every day. Baby would go around me in a large circle at the end of a thirty-foot lunge line. I drove her forward using a lunge whip, which was about six feet long with an eight-foot lash on the end. She walked, trotted, cantered, changed direction, and stopped at a word. She knew the voice commands perfectly: "Walk on, Baby," "Ter-ot, Baby," and "Caaaan-ter," along with "Annnnddd Hoa" to stop and "Change" for her to turn towards me and change direction. She would spiral in and out as I reeled in the line and let it out, always obedient, always happy. She would stand for as long as I wanted.

I ground drove her with her halter so she learned to turn by plow reining. I used the same commands and used the reins as well to add that information into her brain.

The lessons were short but retained. She trusted me more and more each day. A relationship was forming, even against my better judgment. I hadn't planned on another pony. I hadn't wanted another pony. She was living at Sue's. She was Sue's right now.

Still... against my will... I was falling in love little by little. I couldn't help it. Without me even realizing it, she had my heart.

It was now the end of her second year, late fall, my favorite time of year. School had started for the kids. There were fewer lessons when all my summer "out of state riders", and "camp kids" went home. Local kids would get off the bus every night for lessons. Trail rides were on Saturdays. This all left me with plenty of time to train my own "projects."

"Sue, What do you think about starting Baby early?" I asked Sue one day. "She will be three in July and is strong enough. She needs something to do."

Sue and I were eating our favorite lunch together, tuna fish, mayo and onion sandwiches on Wonder Bread. We would wash these down with sugar free hot chocolate. For some reason we don't even know, we latched on to this cuisine. We had been meeting and eating this lunch special for years together at least a couple times a week.

"I think that is a wonderful idea," Sue replied.

And thus, Sue and I decided that it was time to educate Baby-- and time for me to get on her back!

I had already put sacks full of sand on her back while lunging her at the walk and slow trot so I knew she was fine with weight.

I put two lead ropes, one on each side of Baby's halter, and led her across the street, following Sue and her trusty steed. As was my custom training young ones, I planned to get onto her bareback. I found a nice sized rock so I could just stand on it and slip up there onto her back. Baby just stood there, and turned her head to look at me. "What are we doing now?" she seemed to ask. Making sure she was standing square and able to brace against my weight, I put my leg over her back and slid into place right behind her withers. Baby turned her head to sniff at my feet and look up at me. "Hey, how did you get up there?" She seemed to question. I gave her a pat. "What do you think, Baby? Want to go for a ride?" I asked her.

"I think it would be good to just go out the Main Trail and only into the Enchanted Forest this first time," I began by saying.

I just sat quietly for a minute. Baby turned her head to look at Sue and her pony. I then wiggled around on her back, to let Baby get used to the feel of live weight. She lifted her head and put her ears back toward me, but stood firm. When she lowered her head accepting my weight and movement, I said, "Walk on Baby," like I always had on the lunge line. I pushed my seat and squeezed my calves slightly at the same time to give her the feeling that I wanted movement. She took a couple steps, stopped, adjusted her balance, then walked on. She was a little slow at first, but became more confident as she got the idea. She felt solid under me as she began to follow Sue's pony.

"Oh but we have to take her into the OK Corral on our way by, don't you think?" She said as we started down the trail.

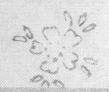

"Well of course," I chuckled "We always have to take a turn or two in the OK Corral when we ride."

At that time, we had a very nice patch of woods across the street from our farm called the Cornwall Nature Preserve. There was such beauty on those trails. Most of the trails were named, and had color coded blobs of paint on the trees lining them.

The preserve was familiar to her, from our many walks, so she willingly began to follow Sue on her very reliable pony into the woods. We started on the Main Trail which began in the parking field at the Cornwall Nature Preserve sign.

This trail had white painted blobs on the trees for people to follow. It went right up the middle of the one hundred sixty acre preserve.

As we started down that pine tree lined path, I was sitting very quietly trying not to unbalance Baby. Within a minute, the woods would pause in a flooded , swampy area where we crossed the first plank bridge. "What a good girl, Baby." I petted her as she crossed the bridge with no fussing at all, just as she had done many times before with me leading her. We continued on up the path where the pine trees would once again line the sides.

Soon we came to the place we called the OK Corral. It was a large almost perfectly round path cut in the woods and to the left of the Main Trail. The circle was wide enough a vehicle and looked like a turn around. There was a small island of bushes, humped up and smack dab in the middle. Looking from above it would have looked like a giant tire. The turnaround was clear of all brush. Not even a blade of grass grew there. It was cool there in the summer and a lot of lessons were taught there on days too hot for the sandy riding ring that had no shade.

We rode inside the OK Corral and rode around to the left, then turned and rode around to the right. We then rode out of the OK Corral and continued on The Main Trail. We next had another small bridge to cross, this time crossing a tiny stream where we would often see fish in the pools below.

The trail once again opened up into a spider web of trails off to the right and left with the Main Trail continuing on up ahead. Here the pines continued on each side. The path itself was smooth and also was wide enough for a vehicle. There was a frog pond nestled in the pines off to the left that had loud, boisterous bull frogs and little peepers in the spring. This time of year, the pond was quiet. Looking to the right was a ridge, lined with birch trees.

As we continued up the trail I leaned forward a little going up a small hill and entered the Enchanted Forest. Here in the summer, I would see colored mushrooms. These red, orange, yellow and purple mushrooms were shaped like Christmas tree lights with stems. There would also be some that looked like flat chocolate chip cookies or pancakes as well as the traditional plain white mushrooms.

The huge pine trees were sparse here, dead and bare except for the tops, which gave an eerie feeling as you rode through as if there were fairies and leprechauns peeking out from behind the tree's massive trunks. We could hear the tree tops squeak and groan in the light breezes. The pine needles from years of falling were deep and spongy. Here is where we turned around, our horses hooves not making a sound.

We rode back the way we had come. This time we didn't go into the OK Corral because that was enough for the first ride. It was about half an hour.

Baby was such an angel and seemed to almost puff herself up as if to say "Look at me, I am finally grown up."

Sue and I kept up a chatty dialog. "Isn't she a good girl?" I said.

"Such a good girl" said Sue in reply.

Baby loved it. I praised her over and over.

When we got back to the parking field, I slid off Baby's back, praising her again and again. I then led Baby and followed Sue across the street back to the barn. "Thank you, Sue, for leading the way," I said as I led Baby into her stall in Sue's barn. I gave Baby several apple slices and a lot more praise. I unhooked the leads and set her free.

We did this routine a few times that fall. Baby was so happy to do anything I asked, always waiting for the treat she knew she would get at the end of each lesson. When she saw a treat, or expected one, she would beg, very loudly, nickering over and over to "say please" while shaking her head up and down, and pawing the floor. This she still does.

OH NO...I AM *NOT* WEARING *THAT*

Baby almost four

Baby's ears flickered and went flat against her head. She snarled, pulled back her lips, and showed her teeth. Her eyes were slits of "watch out, I am angry," and her attitude had changed so quickly from the sweet happy pony to a kicking, pawing, bucking, fighting one. She tried to bite me, snapping and just missing my arm. She stomped her front feet, shook her head from side to side as if to say, "*No!*" and then made that horrible screaming noise, as if in tremendous pain.

I was just trying to tighten her girth.

It was Baby's third autumn, and really time for her to start some routine ring work under saddle. I repeated the lessons she had done the year before, bareback, with a halter, in the woods, with no change in her attitude. I had put the saddle and pad on many times before, so it was a big surprise that she had this reaction to the girth.

"What is wrong with you Baby?" Her action startled me and I quickly took off the saddle and pad before they landed on the floor with her violent action. I checked them over to make sure there was nothing poking her, even brushed the pads underside to make positively sure. I didn't understand. I had put things on her back and had ridden her for almost a year. This didn't make any sense to me.

As I checked everything over, she was eying me as only Baby can. Her ears flicked forward in interest, then flat against her head as she thought about it again. She looked worried. I couldn't figure out why. I could not comfort her with words or pats.

I tried to saddle her again. This time I became angry when she started her tantrum. For the first time in a really long time, I punched her neck and yelled "NO!"

Her ears flipped forward and she was instantly better. Knowing what that word meant, she succumbed to the girth tightening with only a mean face and a click of her teeth. Baby had her own ideas of what being a horse was, and I had others.

I finished getting Baby ready. I was a little apprehensive about riding her after that. I changed my plan from riding in the ring. I decided to take her across the street because it was familiar to her. I got on like I had so many times before from the rock. I didn't use the stirrups just yet because that would have pulled on her girth.

Baby's change was like Dr. Jekyll and Mr. Hyde. She was fine and happy to go out on trail. It was as if the reaction to the girth never happened.

Anytime I tightened the saddle, Baby reacted negatively. After a few difficult sessions, I found a way to work through saddling. At the first sign of defiance, as she put her ears back, I'd shout "Baby, no ears!" Her ears would flip forward and she would ignore the girth.

To this day, Baby doesn't like the saddle being tightened. She will overlook the action, but make sure I see that she doesn't approve of the girth.

The first time I put a snaffle in her mouth, I coated it with molasses and had an apple piece in my hand behind the bit. I let her chew it a while, and let her eat her grain with it for a few nights in her stall, taking it out afterwards. I then ground drove her with it, like I did with the halter. Then I put the halter over her bridle, with a pair of reins on the halter (as always) and a pair on her snaffle. I rode her in this way for a couple of days, using the halter mostly and the snaffle to let her get a feel and get used to it. She didn't mind and maintained a soft mouth that way. I rode her in the snaffle while doing ring work and in her halter on the trails.

Baby almost five, and vicki

With the snaffle and an all-purpose saddle, I did some very light ring work with her. I rode most of the time in just a halter and bareback down the trail. Always only about half an hour as she was still very young.

She was thirteen hands by then, large pony size. A hand measurement being four inches, any horse less than fourteen hands two inches was considered a pony regardless of breed. Baby, being half horse, gave me hope that she would grow a little larger.

In the spring of her fourth year, I started some basic Dressage work, getting her to move away from and bend around my leg, making circles and loops everywhere in the ring. She loved it. It seemed the more

complicated the work, the more she liked it. This kind of work kept her brain much too busy to think of being naughty.

A she progressed, I thought of how much I needed a school pony her size. Banner, a Shetland pony, was nice for the kid's but he was getting very old, had Cushings and he was small for my students who were ready to move on but too afraid to ride the big horses.

I considered asking Sue if I could have Baby back. I didn't think she would mind at all. She had already mentioned that I was welcome to use her for lessons if I wanted.

One day after working Baby, I approached Sue while we were having lunch together. "Sue, I am ready for Baby to come back now. I think she will be good for my kids that are too big for Banner but still afraid of riding the taller horses. I can't imagine she will get out of our new fencing, and she has grown up a lot in her actions these last couple of years."

"I was hoping you would take her back soon," Sue replied excitedly. "My daughter has found some land in South Carolina for me to build on, and I am planning on moving about Christmas time. My doctor said it would be so much better for my asthma in the south. I didn't want to tell you until I knew for sure. And I was wondering what we would do with Baby. I am so glad you are taking her back."

"Oh, Sue, I know you have been talking about South Carolina a lot but I guess I didn't realize that you were actually moving. What are you going to do with your place? And your ponies?" I wondered.

"Well, I was thinking you and Ron might like to buy it and rent it out! And I have looked at a three horse stock trailer and truck to haul with so the ponies can go with me." She brightened.

"We would love to buy your place. Thank you for thinking of us. But I will miss you so very much." I was happy for her, but sad at the same time.

"I will miss you, too," Sue said looking a little sad. "but I really need to move where my breathing will be better. My daughter and son in law have found land and jobs and there is plenty of space for the ponies. We will have twenty acres! You will have to visit us often."

"We will be sure and visit. Maybe even bring horses with us!" I thought about how much fun that could be. "And we must have tuna fish sandwiches and hot chocolate." I chuckled.

"Oh, we will. For sure." She chuckled right back.

"Baby has really come into herself these last couple of years. You can be proud of the work you have done with her," Sue complimented me.

"Well, thank you, Sue. That means a lot to me to have you say that." I said, a tear forming in the corner of my eye. "She sure has given us a run for our money, hasn't she?"

"She sure has," Sue mused.

Sue and me on one of our visits to South Carolina

We have gone to visit Sue and it was wonderful each time. We never did bring our own horses with us on our visits, but we rode every day. Sue would ride Zokeema, and I would ride Jerry. Then we would switch the next day.

On our visits we have gone to Sue's favorite restaurants, met her new friends and for the first time ever we "burned the bird." This is what Sue and her family called deep frying a turkey. It was the best turkey I had ever eaten.

I have missed her a lot over the years. We often call each other to chat, but it isn't the same as our eating tuna fish sandwiches and drinking hot chocolate together.

BABY'S GROWN UP LIFE

The next day, Baby came back. She was so much better as an older pony and got along with most everyone. She still would check out all the hay piles, and she became reunited with Colonel. They shared "the big stall" for a while as I had more horses than I had stalls at the time. I then placed Colonel with one of my adult students, and Baby became more and more independent and sure of herself.

Baby was behaving so well that the next spring I put my first student on her. Anna, who was twelve, had been taking lessons for several years and had ridden all the horses. She also was one of my working students.

Anna got Baby ready with me, and I reminded her about her girthing issues. She had witnessed it many times, but I wanted to make sure she didn't get bitten.

She took Baby into the ring. I stood nearby instructing her. "OK, Anna, warm up as you normally would. Walk around the arena twice then make little circles in every corner. She is used to the work, just not new people riding her." I watched Baby's face very closely to make sure she was happy and wasn't thinking of being naughty. Baby was a lamb.

"Good, Anna." I walked over and snapped the lunge line on Baby and twisted her reins up out of the way. "Now let's do the exercises. I want you to pretend you are a little kid just starting lessons.

"Lets begin with airplane."

Anna put her arms out to the side like an airplane.

"Twist left and look at her tail. Twist right and look at her tail."

Anna did. Baby ignored her.   "OK, Anna. Twist and touch."

Anna, posed in the airplane, bent at the waist and touched each knee with the opposite hand, progressing to each calf, toe and heel. No change in Baby.

She kept walking.

"Anna, reach forward and touch her ears."

When Anna touched Baby's ears, Baby stopped and put her head up a bit. Then she walked on.

"Reach down and give her a hug."

Baby really liked that. She put her head up and down as if using Anna's arms as a scratching post. She kept moving.

This is going well, I thought. "Great. Lie back on her rump and take a nap." Anna bent back and laid her head down on Baby's rump. Baby stopped.

"Walk on, Baby." I said and Baby walked on. "Wonderful, Anna. Lets try around the world." I was lunging to the left so Anna lifted her right leg over Baby's neck, swiveled in the saddle and sat sideways, looking at me. Baby stopped. Anna laughed.

"Walk on Baby" I said.

Baby walked on hesitantly. Anna continued her trip around the world, lifting her left leg over Baby's rump. She was now sitting backwards.

"Scratch her rump, Anna." Anna gave Baby's rump a good scratch.

Baby stopped, lifted her head, stretched out her neck, and top lip. Her tail lifted and she began to move back and forth, enjoying the scratch.

Anna and I laughed at this. "Baby is so funny," Anna said.

"She sure is." I agreed. "Continue around the world."

Anna then lifted her right leg over Baby's rump and sat sideways on the other side. She continued, lifted her left leg over Baby's neck. Once again she was sitting properly in the saddle.

"OK, Anna, you just went around the world, now you have to go home again."

Anna went around the world in the opposite direction to go home. Baby would start to stop each time Anna moved as it felt funny to her to have someone off balance.

"Great! Now lets try flip flops and emergency dismount."

Anna put her hands behind her on the saddle and flipped both her feet up over Baby's neck, clicking her heels together and swinging them down again. Baby stopped and put her head up.

"What was that? Huh, Baby?" I talked to her as if she was a child. "Walk on Baby," I continued.

Baby walked on. She looked a little worried but otherwise was obedient.

"Now the flop part," I coached.

Anna put her hands in front of her on the saddles knee pads and flopped her legs out behind, over Baby's rump, clicking her heels, and swung back again. Baby once again stopped. She swished her tail and humped up her back a little at this.

"Walk on Baby." I said. Baby did. "Now the whole movement, Anna." I prompted.

All in one smooth motion, Anna flipped, flopped and swung both legs over Baby's left side to land on her feet facing the same way Baby was facing.

Baby stopped so quickly Anna almost landed ahead of her.

We both laughed at this. I walked up to Baby and patted her a lot, praising her for at least a half minute. "What a good girl you are, Baby Girl! I am so proud of you." I rubbed her ears and scratched her rump. She loved this.

"OK, Anna, get back on. We will do this again in the other direction and then I will set you lose to finish your lesson. She is doing so well."

The other side was a little easier as Baby was expecting the unbalanced movements. This was very good for Baby. She had passed my test.

I coached Anna as if she was a new student. Since she was helping me train Baby for other riders, her help was valuable.

These exercises were what I had all my little students do to get them over any fear they might have riding. It also taught them that it really isn't that easy to simply tumble off. I asked them of every child that rode with me. I did not ask it of adults as adults are not as limber and it was much harder for them to do them. Kids always had a blast. All my other horses were much older and were all very good with these. Baby needed to learn these things.

Little by little I dared to put more and more kids on her. I first put those who had been riding with me already. Although she was very young to be a school horse, she shined at it. She loved the attention. She truly loved the kids. I always lunged everyone who was new for at least the first few minutes. She never seemed to mind who rode her as long as I was there for her guidance. Lessons on Baby were still less than an hour even with younger lightweight kids on her.

Baby was a very forgiving mount when someone would accidentally kick her or poke her. She never shot forward if kicked by accident like most of the other horses did.

If the kids messages were not clear and she didn't understand what they wanted, she would simply walk over to me, put her brow on my chest as if to say "I don't know what to do, Mum." To me that was very touching and made me realize how much Baby depended on me, that we were connected in a very special way. Most of the time that was when I would put them back on the lunge line for a while. Most of the kids laughed at her antics but some were frightened by them.

For trail riders, I introduced her to the hackamore.

The hackamore is headgear that resembles a halter with shanks. The ones I used at that time had fleece-lined, soft, leather nose bands, a leather chin strap and metal shanks to hold them together. When used, it would squeeze the nose, jaw and behind the ears but not be in the mouth at all. It was stronger than a halter but not as strong as a bit.

She didn't mind this at all. Once again I used Anna as her first rider in the woods, with me walking the first time. I gave her a lesson in the OK Corral.

The reason I used the hackamore was because I didn't want her eating with the bit. I also didn't want the kids or adults to accidentally yank on her mouth if they lost their balance on the uneven trails.   I knew they could not ride in the halter because she was much too strong and would eat the whole time.

With the really young or timid children, I would put anti grazing reins on her as well. These would hook to the bit, or the top of the hackamore shank and back to the saddle D rings. This prevented her to lowering

her head to eat but gave enough freedom for normal movement while riding. The only issue was that she could still reach branches and twigs on the trail. Nothing we could do about that.

If she did walk out of the ring and get her head down in the grass, she was perfectly happy, just to stay there, and ignore the pleading, pulls and kicks of the kids. Then I would say sharply, *"Baby!* You *know* better" and she would lift her head and look at me, (I swear she would smile, and wink). She then would walk back in the ring like nothing happened.

There were times when someone would lose their balance, and Baby would stop and wait for them to right themselves.

It became a game for my more advanced young riders to see who could do an "emergency dismount" before Baby would stop. Since she was very sensitive it was almost impossible to do. It also made her a very safe pony because if anyone began to falter or fall, she would simply stop moving.

Baby was on her way to becoming one of my best school horses.

DON'T LOOK DOWN WHILE RIDING DOWN HILL!

"Don't look down while riding down hill"-- Sometimes it pays to follow my own advice.

It was late fall of Baby's forth year (just before Sue moved south). Baby had been under saddle and working well for more than a year.

I was following Sue through the Cornwall Nature Preserve as usual; we rode together a lot living side by side. We were going to try a new trail for Baby. We had two brook crossings on that particular ride, and I thought it would be good, and time, for Baby to learn to cross them with a rider.

We started as usual on the Main Trail. We had to visit the OK Corral as well. Then right after the second bridge and off to the right was the Brook Trail in red paint. It was a technically difficult trail for beginners. New riders learned how to use their legs and young horses learned to follow trail. A rider might get his knees banged up a bit until he and his horse learned to negotiate it. Bending around trees was a valuable lesson to learn.

This trail went steeply down the first few feet. It followed the brook,which was to the right. This trail went around boulders, and trees, almost touching the water in several places. It was a very low, winding trail with bowed young birch trees on both sides that made a tunnel we would ride through. We called these funny little overhangs chipmunk bridges, thusly named because one of my sons saw a chipmunk run across when were riding under this overhang of trees.

This trail ended in the Enchanted Forest after climbing once more to higher ground. Baby had been on this trail several times and had learned how to pick her way around the large rocks, through the mud and over the little mounds of root infested footing.

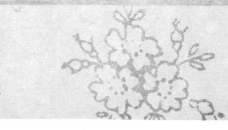

We came to the Enchanted Forest and turned right to cross the first stream crossing. It had a gentle slope down and a steeper grade back up. re was a little snow but the brooks were still liquid and crossable with just a little coating of crunching ice.

After that crossing, we traveled up onto a little ridge with the brook now on our left and several feet below. This trail then took us into a much more dense forest of younger pine trees.   Here Baby grabbed tender shoots of pine needles and chewed them. Green slime flowed from her mouth.

"Is that yummy, Baby?" I asked her. She just chewed contentedly. "Come on,lets go, Piggy Baby." I chuckled. I always found it amazing that she would eat anything green. I also admired her choice of greens. It smelled awesome!

So far she was a willing partner in this new adventure. She loved the trails.

Baby was used to doing what I asked and going pretty much anywhere I asked. She was turning into a very good trail pony. She very rarely spooked.   The first time she did spook was earlier in the season when we happened to come upon two kids on bicycles in the preserve.

The children had been thoughtful and had pulled over to the side to let us pass.

Baby had seen them as predators crouching behind the trees. She'd

stopped, put her head up, then had put her head down. This had given her a good look. I'd felt her tense. She hadn't been sure what it was.

I had nudged her along. "Come on, Baby. It is two kids."

Baby had started sniffing and blowing out her air in a loud snort. The kids had laughed at the funny noise.

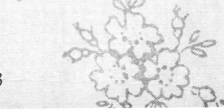

43

"Would you say hi to her please". I asked the kids.

"Hi, horsey," they said in unison.

"Her name is Baby," I had said.

"Hi Baby."

"Can we pet her?" one of the children had asked.

"Not right now," I'd replied. "You can come to the stable later if you would like, but she might step on you here." I had seen they were disappointed, but safety had been my first concern.

Baby still hadn't been sure, even with them talking. "Come on Baby, Walk on." I said a little peeved. I'd given her a strong nudge. She'd taken another deep breath, snorted again, then had slunk down and hurried past trying to get away. It had been so funny and that became how she would handle scary things. It is OK with me. That reaction was much better than spinning and bolting as so many horses do.

There in the nature preserve, Baby had successfully crossed the brook that ended the Enchanted Forest. It had a rather flat landing to it and shallow, very slowly running water. No problem there.

Sue and I had decided beforehand that if all went well, we would leave the preserve and cross onto neighboring property, Willow Farm, the owners of which were friends of Sue.

Another brook separated the farm from the preserve. That particular brook crossing had a rather steep descent into water that was knee deep and flowing much more aggressively than the other brook crossings. The water made waves up against the snow covered, flat topped boulder that was to the right of the trail, half in and half out of the water.

Sue, on her horse went down into the water, crossed, and then waited for Baby and me. Baby didn't even hesitate. She shifted her weight onto her haunches and slid down into the water with her front feet. Then she decided to lower her head, sniff the water and take a drink! With her hind end still up the trail and her front end in the water, this was a very awkward, uncomfortable position for me.

I tipped forward and looked down to wait patiently for her to finish drinking and --I suddenly found myself sliding forward over her neck, saddle and all ! I tried my best to stay upright, not realizing what was happening, but it was impossible! In slow motion, I slipped to the right--right onto the top of the snow covered boulder, flat on my back. My feet were still in the stirrups!

Baby stood still. Her head was caulked to the side to look at me, and her butt was still up in the air. Well, *what are you doing down there?* She seemed to be asking, as she blew on me. She then nuzzled me.

I wiggled my feet out of the stirrups. I was grateful that Baby wasn't easily spooked... and grateful that I didn't end up head first into the cold water!

I started laughing. I looked over at Sue. All I could see was her back. She was bent over her own horse and shaking.

She had witnessed the whole thing and was silently laughing, almost falling off her horse. She wasn't sure if she should laugh or not.   When she realized that I was laughing as well she looked back at me. We both lost it! We just couldn't help it.

"Well," I said between giggles, "that was interesting! What a good pony." Sue agreed, "She sure is good, not to spook at all this."

Baby, with her butt still up in the air on trail and her front end in the water, the saddle on her neck, almost to her ears, stared at me for a just a moment longer.

There was a smile and wink, I swear.

She then very nicely crossed the brook. She found some more pine needles to snack on while she waited for me.

I wore waterproof snowmobile boots, but they wouldn't help me with the water depth. I wiggled down from the boulder into the knee deep brook. The icy water filled my boots as I trekked across.

On the other side, I righted Baby's saddle, and remounted. "Let's ride home." I told Sue who was still giggling. I was wet. I was getting cold. I had enough adventure for one day. I was ready for home.

Going up the bank was a much easier trip, and there was *no* way the saddle was going to slip over her belly. It was then that I vowed to use a crupper the next time we planned a hilly ride. Baby was still young enough that she didn't have much in the way of shoulder muscles or withers. It was a lesson learned for sure. We learn as we go.

A LITTLE HEARTBREAK

Baby had done just about every kind of trail possible, and I really liked how natural it came for her. I thought that Baby would be a good horse for riding Long Distance, competing in either Competitive Trail Rides (CTRs) or possibly even Endurance Races.

CTRs are a timed event of 20-40 miles in one day, averaging about six miles per hour with vet checkpoints along the way. They have a minimum and a maximum time to complete the ride. Horses are scored on condition. The winner is the horse in the best condition at the end of the ride compared to the beginning.

Endurance rides are timed events of 50-100 miles in one day with with less than 50 miles considered limited distance. The are considered races, but are more like marathons, and need to be completed within a maximum time. The first horse to finish is the winner provided they pass the vets' preset "fit to continue" criteria.

In her fifth year, I began training Baby as my personal competition horse for Long Distance. I had competed three other horses in CTRs and found it fun and relaxing. I already felt these qualities riding Baby so I thought, *why not?* The youngest age limit was four years, and she was almost five.

I still used Baby for lessons, but most of her riding time was with me. That winter I started legging her up, with Long Slow Distance (LSD) riding. It would put miles on her but not much stress.

Next we would increase speed but not miles. We went five miles a day, four to five days a week, for several weeks at different speeds no matter the weather. Gradually we added more and more miles. For the first time

I had my farrier put ice shoes on Baby. This would make it possible to ride all winter when the roads and trails were icy.

Very early in the spring, I started timing my treks and keeping track of mileage, speed and making sure she was happy.

Our goal was to average between six and seven miles per hour for sustained work of about four hours across all kinds of terrain. This average speed must account for rests (zero miles per hour), walking during difficult trail conditions, (two-four miles per hour), and make up time with fast trotting or cantering (ten-fourteen miles per hour).

Our first CTR was to be in May in Massachusetts and was called the Apple Blossom 25/50. Riders could choose the one-day twenty-five or two-day fifty mile competition. I chose the two day 50. I had done the ride before and found it a relatively easy ride, appropriate for a novice horse. The terrain in Massachusetts was very flat. Baby and I had been conditioning on hills.

Baby seemed to come alive more with each conditioning ride we did together. I felt we were really a team. A real connection was happening. I knew Baby and she knew me. One word, "Ready?" and she picked up speed.

That spring we had an interruption in our conditioning.

Going down into a brook for water, Baby caught her foot in a hole between two rocks that looked like one solid rock. She went down on her knees while simply trying to continue to walk on. I somersaulted over her head as I looked down to see why she suddenly sank. I landed flat on my back.

It all happened so quickly that by the time I got up, Baby was free of the rocks and was getting her drink. I let her finish then checked her over. I didn't see anything to be concerned about. She hadn't even loosened a shoe. All I could find was a slight scrape on the front of her pastern. I got out my Desitin (something I always carried in my saddle bag) and dabbed a little on her scrape. It would stay on for quite a while because it was waterproof.

I found a few little rocks and filled in the hole so no one else would have that experience, although most horses hooves were bigger than Baby's (flinty hard little mule feet at 00 size), and it was unlikely others would get caught.

I remounted, since she seemed fine, we continued on our ride with me not thinking anything more about it.

When we got back home, I rubbed her down, put liniment and massaged her legs. She did her "carrot stretches," which she loved.

We had gone about forty miles over the weekend so I gave her four days off completely. The remainder of the week I just used her for little kid lunge lessons and pony rides at a walk while they did exercises. This would keep her limber.

I got Baby ready and started riding the next Saturday, a week after our mishap at the brook. I felt she was off a little, not much, but just enough for me to feel it. I asked others riding with me if they could see where she was lame. I couldn't figure out where she was lame, it was so subtle. No one else could see that she was lame at all. I could feel she wasn't moving in her normal way; her gait was off.

There was no swelling, no heat anywhere on her body, and no soreness that I could detect. She was normal otherwise.

I trailered her to an equine clinic. I trotted her out while the veterinarian watched. Then she did all the traditional testing in order to identify the lameness, such as flexion, palpations, X-rays. She could not put a finger on it either and recommended we see the equine orthopedic surgeon.

The next week the surgeon looked at her X-rays and repeated some of the same lameness tests. During the trot out, she proved very lame on the left fore when flexed and trotted. All he saw on the X-rays was that the cartilage was a little shorter in the left pastern than the right one.

"Baby has Juvenile Arthritis." he concluded. "She will probably never be completely sound."

I cried on the way home. I was heartbroken. I had such regal plans for Long Distance. This diagnoses shattered those dreams.

At home, I gave Baby a great big hug and set her free in the pasture. She limped sulkily away. With this permanent diagnoses, I didn't know what to do with her. Perhaps a walk-trot school pony for my little students? In the mean time she would rest as I was instructed as I didn't want to cause her any pain and I started the recommended joint supplements. I would get another horse for my for my distance riding and Baby was to just be.

DEPENDABLE SCHOOL HORSE

Student cantering

Two months later, I watched as Smokey, my new long distance horse, chased Baby around in the paddock. She was not limping! I could not believe it. I thought maybe the supplements *were* working that well. I took her off them so I could observe her.

Baby continued to be pain free and sound as I kept an eye on her. I watched her in the paddock. She needed to work. I started very lightly working her again. First with small children, then with my older ones. Once again she blossomed as student after student rode her and fell in love with her.

After a few months' work with Baby staying sound, I thought maybe she was sound enough for adults to ride in beginner lessons.

I started riding her again very gently. I continued her schooling in dressage and after a few weeks, I held my breath as I added a little jumping to her schooling. She had been trotting ground poles for a while now with the kids with no problems at all. She stayed sound. I wanted her as versatile as my other school horses. I had adults that really wanted to ride smaller horses.

I got a call from the local human resources program director and was asked if I took handicapped children for lessons. I explained that I was not trained in that field but was willing to try. With this opportunity I branched out and gave lessons to handicapped children. Baby was very patient and sympathetic. She seemed to know just how important it was to be on her best behavior. She soon won the reputation of a super pony for that. There were several handicapped children as well as two adults that rode her regularly and would request her over the bigger horses.

I found that children with Autism especially blossomed while riding her. One such child, Johnny, who was seven, had ridden Baby several times in the ring. After ring time, it was my custom to take students out on the trail, me on foot, to cool off their horse in the shady trail out to the OK Coral. As with all my students, he loved going out on trail. When he was confident and I felt he could rein Baby as she ambled along behind me and Smokey, I started taking him out on trail every other lesson.

Almost home on this bright summer day, I heard "help" in a very soft voice. I looked behind me. There was Baby, eating twigs, just as undisturbed as could be. But the little boy was hanging upside down by one stirrup.

I flew off Smokey and rushed to the students aide. Johnny had his other leg was sticking straight up in the air, his hands were almost touching the ground. His toes kept him from completely falling.

"What happened?" I said after getting him back up into the saddle.

"I grabbed a tree and Baby didn't stop in time, so I fell." he told me.

Baby had been able to feel when Johnny was off balance. Instead of spooking at him when he fell she simply stopped. Baby, such a good girl, simply saw an opportunity to eat. This calmness and sensitivity to her rider made her a dependable school horse.

Baby became my most valued and dependable school horse. I began to say "She is worth her weight in gold!" Even though she was a pony in hight (being 13.2 with very short legs) she was a horse in body size and as long as you didn't look down, you felt like you were on a horse. I had a lot of people request her to ride *because* she was small enough to get on. Being close to the ground, falling wasn't something to be a afraid of. Baby was a very smooth ride being easy gated.

TRICKS ON A DRESSAGE RIDER

I had riders from all walks of life come and ride with me over the years, but Baby wasn't quite as sympathetic to perfectly able adults as she was with children or the handicapped.

One year I had an out of state rider take a few lessons while she was visiting in the area. Sandy rode Dressage and had a horse back home. She had only ridden in an indoor ring and wanted to ride outside and take a few trail rides as well.

I gave her a little information about each horse I had at the time, and she chose to ride Baby that day. Baby was totally opposite of her own horse, which was a tall Thoroughbred. She groomed and tacked up, even laughing at Baby's antics as I held her head for the girth. I gave her a little information about each horse I had at the time, and she chose to ride Baby that day. Baby was totally opposite of her own horse, which was a tall Thoroughbred. She groomed and tacked up, even laughed at Baby's antics as I held her head for the girth.

Since Sandy was a Dressage rider with a regular trainer, I asked her to warm up the way she had learned. With new, experienced riders, I like to watch their routine warm up. Usually I can tell what type of lessons they are accustomed along with their experience level.

As I watched Sandy's riding to get a feel of what we could work on in the first lesson, I gave her a run down about Baby's habits and her love of grass, mentioning that she should be on her toes, to not let the reins slacken at all, and to keep Baby between her seat, hands and legs.

My riding ring was a small Dressage arena, twenty by forty meters, which bordered the pasture on one of its long sides. I had various letters around the school marking points on a Dressage test, including "A" at the top on of the arena on the short side, and "C" at the lower end bordering the green lawn beside my house.

After warming up, as Sandy trotted around the outside of the arena, I began instruction. "Sandy, come down the center line from A towards me." I was standing at X, which was the middle of the arena. "Keep straight and continue on to C."

Sandy nodded and headed Baby down the center of the arena the long way. As she went by me, I continued, "Then make a left turn. Go into the corner and back up across the diagonal to change direction.

She did as I asked, bending Baby around her leg at the corner of the arena. "Lengthen the stride, Sandy," I continued. "Bend into the corner and continue around the whole school."

Sandy did well following my instruction, but on the long side of the arena, I noticed that her reins had become a little slack. I reminded her, "Take up the reins—remember contact—and push her into the corner to bend her, keeping the outside rein but flexing with the inside." I continued, "Keep that bend, and when you get to C, make a full circle of twenty meters." That was about sixty six feet. "

Sandy had her reins collected again, looking determinedly through Baby's ears.

I told her, "Think of riding a quarter of a circle at a time, just kiss the track, continue on and kiss X in the middle , kiss the track and back to C."

As she was just coming to X, I asked her, "Try another circle as that one was a little square."

All looked good until I noticed that her reins once again had become a little slack. I saw Baby's little, evil, laughing eye as she looked right at me. My rider was too relaxed and thought Baby was on autopilot. Baby took full advantage of the moment.

Before I could say "contact," Baby trotted, pretty as you please, over the rail road tie that marked the end of the ring as if it were simply a ground pole.

She suddenly stopped and buried her head into the lawn! Sandy shot over her head, somersaulting onto her back in the grass, reins still in her hands. I couldn't do anything but watch as I began to run to her aid.

"Sandy, are you OK?" I asked, running over to her and trying my best not to laugh. I made sure she wasn't hurt.

She stood up and looked bewildered and said, "I have never had that happen before!"

Seeing she was all right, I lost it. I started laughing so hard. She had no choice but to join me.

In between bursts of laughter she said, "I see what you mean about keeping a contact on her. I guess she showed me a thing or two. OK, let's try that again. This time I will not let her get the upper hand."

When we stopped laughing, she said. "It is quite different to ride in the open than in an indoor. This is really good for me to learn."

We continued her lesson. This time Sandy made sure to keep contact. She came back several times that summer and throughout the following years—but Baby never got another chance to eat with that rider.

STARTING HER ENDURANCE CAREER

Aimee getting ready for her fist endurance ride

I had many students pass through and ride Baby, not only children, but also adults. Baby was always happiest on trail.

One such young student was very talented and had such a good time riding that I started doing more and more with her and Baby. Her name was Aimee, and I would take her with me when we trailered places

to ride. She expressed an interest in doing a long distance ride with me. She wanted to do an endurance ride that was fifty miles long. I was entered in the two day hundred with King. (Smokey had died of an abdominal aneurysm and I had bought King.)

I thought for a while about Baby doing long distance. I hadn't thought about it at all since Baby was lame three years earlier. I was a little apprehensive as I was so afraid that the lameness would recur. I also wanted to be her rider on her first ride. I wasn't sure how I felt about it. I hadn't thought about riding her in competition since she had become lame. I had King now for that. Baby was valuable as my most trusted school horse.

I decided that it was not a bad thing to have her first competition with a junior. After all, I had King as my personal riding horse now and was rarely riding Baby any more. She was very busy with all my lesson kids.

So Aimee and I trained a little harder than we would normally train as I didn't want the heartbreak of her being pulled in a ride with one of my students on her. It would be a big blow to a young girl, I was sure. If she became lame on a training ride, then that was that! She would simply not do long distance rides.

Baby was keeping up with me and King just fine with no problems at all. She drank and ate where she should, stood still to be handled while we practiced her "hands on" part of the exam, and Aimee was a very dedicated rider coming several times a week to ride and make sure she herself was also in shape for it.

She learned how to cool Baby off, how to sponge on the go, how to feed her, groom her, bathe her, and rub her down.

I gave Aimee's family a run down on the care of Baby at each hold. Aimee had a real crew. Her whole family was at her beck and call. They would take care of Baby as well as Aimee. We were ready.

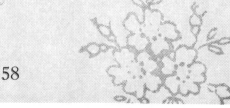

There was a great amount of excitement. As always, Ron was my "crew," and he was all I needed for a crew. He knew what I wanted and when while on a ride.

So Baby, at eight years old, and Aimee, at ten, were going to do their first Long Distance ride, the Northeast Challenge 50/100 Mile Endurance Ride. That competition was not what a typical pick for a first Long Distance ride. An easier starting point was a ride half that and a Competitive Trail Ride (which is less intense) instead of Endurance.

They would follow me and King on the first day of our two-day 100 mile ride.

Four thirty that morning, I woke my little rider up so she could do her share of feeding and make sure she got breakfast as well. An hour later, we tacked up and walked our horses around to warm up as the ride was to start at six with a starter's gun.

We mounted and rode down the trail in the opposite direction away from the excitement. It was nearing six, and I wanted to make sure both horses were calm. We planned to leave after the pack left and start out slowly.

We were warming up away from the crowd of riders when the starter's gun went off. The herd of about thirty-five excited horses and riders exploded in tight group.

I cringed seeing them leave in such a fashion. In my opinion, it would have been an invitation to be kicked. I was glad that we were at a safe distance from them. Some of the horses were bucking, rearing and hopping down the start of the ride.

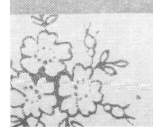

King was also bucking and hopping while I force him to wait. Starting with everyone would have been too much excitement for him, and I might have lost track of Aimee and Baby.

We waited a minute or two longer until I was sure we had an open space to start our ride calmly.

We began trotting, and we were on our way. I have done this many times so I was not nervous but my little student was. Aimee was already talking constantly and extremely excited. Baby just took it all in stride. To her it was like any other ride we had done, just King and her and me and Aimee.

King knew the difference and he was high. He performed "airs above the ground"! I was accustomed to his silliness—it was competition that was nerve racking, it was trying to stay in my saddle! He was such a foolish boy.

As we rode by the starter and the crowd of onlookers and pit crews, I heard King's previous owner yell to me, "Vicki, make sure you have your Velcro tight!" She simply meant "don't let him dump you." She had King's father and knew what I was feeling as he crow hopped, darted and jerked down the road.

We continued on down the dirt road, a road we have ridden on many times before while getting ready for this ride. We came upon a rider who had decided to get off and walk until her horse calmed down. In endurance riders are allowed to get off and walk or run whenever they want or need. We passed and wished her well. Her horse was young and this was his first Endurance race as well.

To me, Endurance is more of a marathon rather than a race. I have never been very competitive. I just enjoy the ride and like to see what my horse and I can do together as a team for it is very much teamwork for horse and rider.

First vet check went very well. We un-tacked and sponged down the horses to cool them. We didn't let them eat yet as that would have pushed up their pulse a bit. The trick is to keep them as quiet as possible until they pass the pulse and respiration part (P&R). Both horses pass the P&Rs and the trot out (checking for lameness) as the vets watch. They both stood quietly while they were prodded, poked, and pinched (to check for dehydration, soreness or tight muscles) and make sure there are plenty of gut sounds coming from their bellies.

When she finally was allowed to eat, Baby ate like she had never had food before. This was typical for her. King never had been a very good eater, but he did eat most of the mash I had prepared beforehand for him and accepted the electrolytes that I had mixed with applesauce. This I squirted into his mouth with a giant syringe.

I gave Baby her electrolytes as I wanted to make sure this part had been done correctly. She thought of it as candy and opened her own mouth, very happy to have 'special stuff', and soaking up all this attention. Such a ham!

We then handed the horses to our crews and got something to eat ourselves. I looked around and realized that several of the "hot shots" had been pulled and would not continue this ride.

Often when people let their horses start out too fast, racing the first few miles, they burn out fast, have either lameness or metabolic issues, and the vets will pull them from the ride. The vets will not allow a horse they think might be in metabolic trouble or end up too lame to continue. Other times people simply decide that it is enough for them today. Some riders understand. Others rebel and ridicule the vets as their idea of

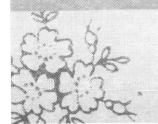

grandeur is to "win this race." It doesn't do any good to win the first fifteen miles when the ride is fifty or one hundred miles. Some just don't understand that.

Our waiting time was up soon. We offered water one more time to the horses, tacked up, climbed aboard, handed our time slip to the time keeper, and we are cleared to go.

"Ready?" I asked Aimee.

"Yup," she replied. Then we were on our way.

The second and third vet checks went similar to the first with more horses pulled but with ours still "good to go."

Aimee was beginning to get a little tired. It was an emotional/mental tiredness since we had only ridden this far (by now thirty miles) twice over the last few months. To avoid over training, you rarely ride the full distance of an endurance ride. Instead you ride a shorter version only faster than you plan to compete.

The fourth and last vet checks were back at camp with only a five mile loop left to go. By then Aimee was very tired. This was farther than she had ever gone before. Baby still looked fresh and fabulous. She was still happy to go. I am sure she thought of this ride as an all you can eat salad bar. King was fine physically, but didn't want to leave camp, as camp meant rest to him.

I told Aimee, "Only five more miles, you can do it."

She perked up, got a little smile on her face, and we started back down the dirt road for the last time that day.

We picked up a slow canter. By now we had passed many riders and quite a few have been pulled. I felt fortunate that we had escaped any metabolic or lameness issues; it can happen to any horse at any time.

We made the loop and came cantering across the finish line to claps, yahoos and smiles on the faces of all who were there to see us complete.

Aimee started to cry as it hit her that she has finished riding fifty miles. This is an emotional time for all who experience it for the first time. It was especially so for a little girl of ten.

At the after ride dinner and awards, Aimee found out that she had won top ten junior. Baby won rookie horse. Aimee also won rookie rider (against adults as well). She went home a happy, satisfied, and very tired little girl.

For me, the moment was secretly bitter sweet. I wanted to ride Baby in her first Long Distance ride, but was so very happy that a little girl's dreams came true.

I had another day to ride, so Ron took Baby home for a well-deserved week off.

Baby had at last proven herself as a Long Distance horse!

.Aimee and Baby.

ENTER ABBY

Abby came to ride with me about a year after Baby's debut as a Long Distance horse.

Abby was a tall girl at thirteen. She was very shy. I introduced her to Baby. I thought that Baby would be a good one for her to ride the first time. Baby was just small enough not to intimidate a new rider.

Abby climbed up on the mounting block, put her left foot in the stirrup and in her excitement to ride hoisted herself up and almost all the way over Baby's back! I was holding the off stirrup so was able to catch her and right her back up.

Her first lesson was on the lunge line as that was how all my students started out. When time came to dismount, I coached her on how to do it. Her right leg didn't seem to want to come with her left leg, but because Baby was short and Abby tall it turned out OK. She touched down with her left, the right slipped right down at the same time. I got on and demonstrated how to properly get off, but thought maybe next time I would use Boy. He was much more substantial and much wider, lowering the chance of slipping over to the other side when mounting, and maybe more steady to get off from as well.

Abby made out really well getting on Boy. He stood for her and as she hoisted herself once again from the mounting block, he was much steadier and she landed perfectly in the saddle. Again she was lunged, but at the end of the lesson she rode by herself.

With Boy, getting on was much easier but getting off was much harder. She would try to get both legs over to the left like I had demonstrated, but for some reason her right leg got left behind and stuck on the back of the saddle as her left foot came out of the stirrup.

Boy, being the patient horse he was, just stood still. It was scary for me to watch her struggles to get off, and once on the way down I was helpless to help her other than to push her right leg over. Getting both legs on the left side of the horse just seemed not to want to happen.

I wondered if it seemed that Boy was a long way from the ground (he was almost two hands taller than Baby) or that the possibility of a fall when both legs were on the same side was in the back of her mind.

She didn't have any trouble getting off Baby.

My decision for her to ride Baby was a selfish one. I decided I would rather she have a little trouble getting on than getting off. On her next lesson we spent a good amount of it on mounting and dismounting. It worked! By the end of that lesson, Abby was confident enough to get off properly.

Also by then, Abby and Baby had formed a bond.

Baby and Abby hit it off right away. Baby took care of Abby and she adored Baby, coming to the barn on her non riding days just to be near her and groom. What better place for a teenage girl to be than at a barn full of horses?

Abby was thirsty for horsey knowledge. I was very happy to oblige.

One rainy lesson day, too rainy to ride, Abby still wanted to come to the barn. That day I taught Abby to "super groom" Baby. With Abby's care, Baby was always shiny and trimmed. Baby was also always "well treated" (got a lot of treats) when Abby was around.

My version of super groom was long and hard. Starting with a soft curry, the horse was curried, using a lot of elbow grease, in large circles over her whole body. This brought the dirt and dust out of the skin and into the coat. It also helped to distribute the natural oils, which Baby has an abundance.

Next was a stiff brush to "flick" off the dirt. Starting just below the jowls, since the brush is too harsh for the face, I brushed the same area three or four times, cleaning the brush with fingers before moving on to the next area. Always brushing in the direction of hair growth was difficult on Baby. She had a lot of swirls and cowlicks. Making sure her belly and all the way down her legs get "flicked" was very important. At the end of the leg, a swipe behind each pastern was needed to remove any crusted mud. This helped to prevent any soreness or the mean fungal growth that is commonly called scratches.

Next I took the softer brush and swiped, cleaned brush, swiped, cleaned brush in this manner all over the horse until the horse shined. This brush could also be used on the face, but I usually had smaller ones for that. Brushing the face and inside the ears was very important to Baby. She loved this. This also let me know if biting insects managed to get past the fly spray into her ears.

Then I brushed through the mane and tail with either a stiff brush or a mane and tail comb. Spritzing the tail first with a conditioner helped with the tangles.

Cleaning the hooves was a challenge to some kids. Although Baby was good about picking up her feet, she tended to then lean on the slower person while she snoozed on the cross ties.

A wet towel took away the goop from the eyes, inside the ears, and cleaned under the tail and between the legs. These areas often got a buildup of smegma (body oil and dirt) that could itch and be uncomfortable.

Lastly, I took another towel and "strapped" Baby, which was pleasurable to the horse and muscle work for the groomer. Either dry or very slightly damp, I wound it around my fist and, starting at just behind the head, I put a little power into it to massage the muscles as I swiped. Staying off the bones was a must because this could hurt the horse, but she really enjoyed the muscles being "pounded" in this way. It also puts a really nice shine on the coat.

I always had a saying at my barn: "If your arms are not tired when you are finished, you didn't groom well enough." This usually made the kids laugh.

Abby was so enthusiastic that I asked her dad if she could come more often and help me for extra ride time. Since they lived just a couple miles up the road, it was convenient for her to get off the bus at my place, which most of my students did anyway during the school year.

Abby mentioned that she was interested in showing. I hadn't shown in years but looked up some of the local schooling Dressage shows. I started concentrating on Dressage for her first show. We worked on all the movements of the tests but not in the order they would be at the show so that the horse wouldn't learn the order of the movements and expect them.

Abby and I practiced her tests on foot in my living room, putting up paper letters and "walked, trotted and cantered" where appropriate. Over the years, I did this with many of my students, and it is a wonder that my living room carpet didn't have holes where we worked so hard on our tests.

Abby had practiced and practiced until she knew her tests perfectly. She and Baby were ready for their first Dressage show!

Abby and Baby at their first Dressage show

Abby was at the barn at the break of dawn on show day. I told her to dress in her show clothes, but put other clothes over so she would be ready quickly when the time came for her classes.

Although we arrived early to watch others, Abby was very nervous and worried that she wouldn't do well. She was not sure about all the people watching.

"Abby, just pretend it is just you and me in the ring. Block out everyone else. Do this for fun! You are just going to run through your tests. Just like at home. Only you will be riding this time." I became her stern teacher right then.

"OK, I will try," she said in a little, shaky voice.

Baby didn't care what was happening. She is such a level headed pony that to her it was simply a bunch of horses milling around, and as long as there was green grass to eat, nothing else mattered.

Together we tacked Baby. She had been groomed within an inch of her life at the barn and was shiny and clean. Hoof oil had been applied to her hooves and baby oil to her muzzle and around her eyes to make them stand out. Her tail had conditioner in it so it sparkled. And since she had no mane to speak of, we didn't have to worry about that, except to even it out a bit. Her tack had been cleaned and her bit polished. I used toothpaste for bit polish. I thought of it as less toxic than the traditional metal polish.

Abby took off her outer clothes. She had dressed in her black breeches, paddock boots and white blouse. With her long wavy hair tied back, she looked beautiful and was ready for her first class. I watched and coached as she warmed up in the warm up ring. All competitors had numbered cards with hooks for placing on the horses bridles. We kept an eye on the riders scheduled before her so we would be ready when the rider just before her left the ring. Then the rider before Abby finished.

The bell rang for the one minute warning to get into the ring. I had just a moment to give last minute advise. I took a deep breath as I led her up to the ring entrance.

"You will do wonderful. Don't pay any attention to the onlookers or other horses. Go deep into your corners as you have learned. Judges love to see riders go deep into the corners." I started to drill her as is my nature.

"OK," was all Abby said. I could see she was terrified and not thinking of what I was saying, which was probably too much at this time.

I took a deep breath and I paused for a moment, remembering my first show. I had never gotten to show as a child. I'd never even took lessons. I'd had to wait until I was eighteen before my first show. I had ridden other people's horses in Saddle Seat, Western Pleasure, and Hunt Seat at the county fair shows. It hadn't been until I was in my twenties that I took lessons and showed in Dressage and Eventing. For some reason, I have never been shy or afraid at shows, but I remembered there had been others who had the same look Abby had right then.

It gave me an idea for Abby.

"Abby, just have fun!" I finally said.

"OK," she said. This time she smiled.

As Abby went down the center line to begin her test, I stepped back from the arena. It was out of my control now. I crossed my fingers and hoped she would remember her test.

Abby was tense riding at first, and Baby felt her tension. They performed the movements in order, but did so awkwardly. The came down the diagonal of the arena, but they passed through X and Abby did not change the diagonal she was posting. Suddenly, she looked up and made eye contact with me. Her eyes brightened as she remembered.

Abby changed her diagonal. I think my presence took her back to our ring work, and she began to look around for the letters and ride. I visibly saw her relax.

She and Baby did wonderfully! Great success for her first show.

I took her to two more Dressage shows that summer. She and Baby did very well, but Abby wasn't sure that was what she really wanted to do. She liked riding in the ring, but she liked trail riding better.

Abby and Baby became such a good team. They had such joy in each other.

Abby and I were becoming closer with each ride we took together. It was more of a friend than just a student.

"Abby, would you like to try a Competitive Trail Ride?" I asked her while on one of our many trail rides.

"What is that like?" she asked me.

"It is just trail riding, but your horse is judged on condition as you ride." I told her.

She jumped at the chance. It was then that Baby really shined. She and Abby were an item. They rode not only with me but with a friend, Heather, who was close to her age. Heather lived across the Nature Preserve. Heather's horse at the time was Lady. So Heather and Lady and Abby and Baby would ride together at least twice a week. They had quite the adventures.

Abby and I would ride together a couple times per week as well. Baby got into really good shape with no lameness problems at all.

We had so much fun together and most of the stories in the rest of the book are with me and Abby riding together with various friends, getting ready for CTRs and Endurance rides.

Abby went to many CTRs and Endurance rides with Baby over the next few years.

In 1999, they not only won a versatility award from Eastern Competitive Trail Ride Association (ECTRA) but also won Junior Reserve Grand Champion for the whole East Coast. That was a very proud moment for not only Abby but for me as well. I was so proud of Abby's accomplishments. She had gone from a timid, shy, gangly teenager to a confident, accomplished rider in such a short time.

I was even more proud that the grumpy little horse I raised turned out to be such a good horse. Sound in limb and sane of mind—she is still grumpy!

We had a little celebration at the house and invited Abby's whole family. She still has that trophy! It is a beautiful head bust of a horse carved in wood.

We have had many fun rides together.

Abby and Baby waiting in line to go out on Maine 80

All done for the day.

EASY BOOT BRIDGE

"OK, girls, tell me the joke," I said.

They continued laughing, almost out of breath, they were laughing so hard.

"What is wrong with you girls? What is so funny?"

That particular day was extremely hot and humid, and I had only coaxed Abby, Kara (another of my students who routinely rode Boy) and Heather to go with me on our weekly long ride. Other students and friends thought it was just too hot to go riding.

We took a trail ride that we all really liked on hot, steamy days because this particular ride crossed the river several times.[no paragraph break] During the river crossings, we would let the horses stand and drink in the water after we sponged them while we had water fights. We filled our sponges and would swing them at each other, making water spray all over us. It was a fun, cool way to spend our time. Then we would finish crossing to the other side to continue our ride.

One such crossing had been muddy on one side. The deepest water was up to the bigger horses' bellies. That meant it went most of the way up Baby's saddle.

"Lift your feet over Baby's neck Abby," I had reminded her. The saddle was synthetic but her boots were not.

We had to ride beneath a suspended snowmobile bridge to get to the other side. It touched the ground on either side of the river in an arch that hung on cables and chains. Often snowmobile bridges are made so that the snow will fall through in between the planks. Usually the space was big enough for a horse's hoof to

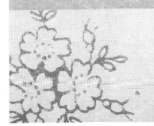

get caught and go through, so we avoided bridges that we knew were built this way. Since this one was also suspended, that meant it would swing and bounce when crossed.

So into the water, then under the bridge we had gone. We waded across and up a steep, slippery bank on the other side. We only crossed it in that direction because the bank was much too steep and slippery to go down *into* the river on horseback. We would eventually come out on another trail to go back home, making a large circle.

We had scrambled to the top and continued on our way, the trail opening up into a sandpit with a network of roads going through and into the woods where the rest of our beautiful trails were.

"Everybody ready to trot?" I had asked.

"Yes!" they had all said together.

We had picked up a trot and for a couple strides, I had wondered why King was trotting funny.

"Girls, can you see anything funny about King's legs?"

"No" had come in unison.

Even though I had believed them, I'd had to look down at King's feet, "Oh man, I have lost an Easy Boot. No one saw it come off?" Easy boots were rubber boots that replaced shoes, and I was experimenting with them on King.

No, they had not seen it come off, so it had meant going back, riding slowly, and looking right and left the whole way back to the river to see where I might have lost it. Perhaps it had been flung in the woods.

We hadn't seen it on the side of the trail. We hadn't seen it on the trail.

"Maybe you lost it in that deep mud before we crossed the river; it was pretty muddy there," Heather had said.

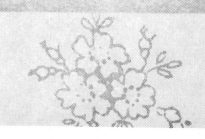

"Oh I hope not. I'll never find it in that mud," I had said, but in my gut, I had known she was right. The heavy mud would suctioned the boot right off King's hoof.

Back to the river we had gone.

I had gotten off King and had tied him to a tree. "I will be right back," I had said, "will you watch King for me?"

"Yup, we will let the horses eat while you check," Kara had replied.

I had thought about taking off my boots but remembered the slippery rocks and considered the possibility of fishing hooks in the river.

I then proceed to climb down the bank--remember I said it was steep and slippery? I slid on my butt all the way down to the river, cold and wet and waist deep.

"Woo! This is *cold*!" I had yelled to the girls, and I had continued across to the muddy part on the other side, looking into the water the whole way trying to find my Easy Boot. It was black and would not be easy to find.

All the way on the other side, I had spotted it. It was sitting there just where we would have entered the river. Evidentially the mud had sucked it off. I held it up and yelled "Hurray! I found it!" It might not seem like a big deal to lose a rubber boot, but those babies were expensive, so it had been good to find it.

Then I had heard the girls' laughter echo across the river. *What's up with that? What is wrong with those girls?* I had wanted in on the joke.

I had retraced my steps back across the river. I crawled up the bank only to fall back into the water two more times before making it up the bank.

Now I stood dripping wet with all three girls around me laughing hysterically.

I repeated my question, "What's so funny?"

"What is wrong with you girls? What is so funny?" I am laughing myself by now as it is catching.

Abby, the only one who could stop laughing long enough to talk, said, "We were just wondering why you didn't use the bridge." Gotta love those girls.

I looked at the bridge, looked at the girls, looked back at the river, and back at the girls.

"Well dah," I said. This brought on a new round of hysterical laughter.

That bridge has been dubbed "Easy Boot Bridge," and this story is usually told at my expense by these three girls for a good laugh.

It is good sometimes to goof up in front of students and young friends to show that even teachers and um..older adults are not perfect. It is also good to have a very good sense of humor when dealing with horses and kids.

I put back on Kings Easy Boot when my laughing subsided.

We were all in high spirits that day as we continued our ride. We rode through the sand pit, into the cool pine tree lined woods, trotting and cantering up and down the hills on the paths and cooling off in several other river and brook crossings before coming out onto the main road and back up the hill to home. Over and over again the girls would start laughing, and I couldn't help but join them. We all went home feeling like special friendships were made that day and I believe there were. This was one of those days that I felt like a kid myself, living my dream of a horse lover and having such good lifetime friendships.

HIGH TIDE !

Abby and Baby at the ocean

"What do you mean go to the beach? But it is winter! We can't swim in the winter!" Abby looked at me

curiously as she unbuckled the girth on Baby's saddle.

We had had many riding adventures together. Me and whoever wanted to go along. Usually at least one

student, perhaps a friend or two. As a rule, they were all day trail rides, but it was still winter so riding for

long periods of time was very limited and depended on the footing and weather. Tomorrow promised to be

an unseasonably warm winter day. The weatherman promised high fifties. It was February vacation and there was no school. I thought it would be fun to take Abby and Kara, another of my students. To the beach to ride. Lynn, a friend of mine who also had a trailer, offered to trailer one of them along with her horse.

Equestrians are allowed to ride on our Maine beaches from October 15th to May 1st.

Kara had been riding with me for a little longer than Abby and they liked each others company.

There was a bright blue sky, the sun was toasty warm, there was a slow salty breath of ocean air, and sea gulls were welcoming us as we pulled into the parking space, at Pine Point.

I started to get excited, "The sweet ocean is calling us. Lets tack up quickly so we can take advantage of the lowest of low tides."

The girls were chatting, a little giddy, as we rode down to the deep, soft, *brown sugar* beach. The ocean sand seldom freezes in winter so there was no snow or ice to hinder our ride. King, my gray Arabian, and Lynn's tall black grade horse, had been to the beach many times, however Baby and Boy ,a bright chestnut Quarter Horse I owned, had never been.

As we continued down to the water (where the footing is firm) Baby , who is usually unflappable, tried not to get anywhere near those monster waves. She wanted nothing to do with that moving water and she snorted and backed up just as fast as her little legs would take her, backwards, up the beach and into the deep sand. This was a new experience for Abby as Baby is usually so well behaved.

Boy, though, was fine with the water and all its movements and went on in, standing contentedly, while the gentle waves curled around his legs.

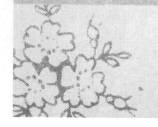

"Abby," I yelled. "Bring her over and back her into the water with Boy."

Lynn and I couldn't help but laugh as Baby kicked at the waves with both hind feet as the waves touched her. She snorted and pranced, tail and head as high as she could get it trying to see what was behind her and trying not to touch the water with those little hooves. I could see that Abby was a little afraid but had confidence that she was safe. Finally, Abby got the little horse into the water.

"Good job, Abby," I told her. "Give her lots of pats and tell her how good she is".

Baby no longer attacked the waves, but she kept a cautious eye on them, turning her head sideways, with her ear cocked toward the water, shaking all the while.

Distracted by Baby's silliness, I wasn't paying attention to my own horse, who decided it would be fun to lay down and roll in the water. "King! *no!*" I dug my heels into him and moved him forward, just barely stopping him from dropping me in the cold ocean water.

I looked up at my fellow riders, who were laughing hysterically at me, and said, "I guess we better get riding before I end up in the water! Want to ride to the pier and back? It is about four miles to the pier, so eight miles would be good to let King run a bit before he starts acting up." King got bored easily and had a habit of finding exciting things to do like suddenly taking off at a dead gallop and taking me on an unplanned turbo speed bronco ride.

After warming up at the trot for a few minutes, King started to canter in place.

"Everyone ready to go?" I ask.

"No, you go ahead. King needs the work. I think I will just putter along." Says Lynn.

"Me too, I will stay with Lynn." said Kara.

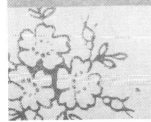

"Come on Abby. What do you think? You want to canter? Or stay with Lynn and Kara?." I invited.

"I will go with you and King." she said

"OK then, lets go." I let King canter forward. He was ready to go.

"I have never ridden so fast before." Abby said, out of breath as we rode to the pier. We slowed down to a trot. Baby, almost two hands shorter than King didn't have any trouble keeping up. Both horses were still fit from the summer before of endurance and competitive trail competitions.

"That was a gallop," I informed her. "Isn't this fun?"

"So much fun!" She replied excitedly. "I have never galloped before. That was really fast, and a little scary."

Lynn and Kara were content to putter along behind us, and were only tiny dots when Abby and I reached the pier. Abby and I played in the sand waiting for them to catch up. We made circles, serpentines and other figures with me instructing as we rode side by side. Sort of a funny looking drill team.

"Try to stay right beside me as we circle, just barely touching our stirrups the whole time," I told her.

"Can we try a figure eight?" she asked.

"Yup, lets try that, on one circle I will be on the outside, and the other half of the eight you will be on the outside, and we'll try to make two complete circles the same size and joined in the middle."

It was so much easier in the vast openness we had at the beach then in the confinements of a ring and we tried over and over again to make that figure eight and not crash into each other with King on a tight rein, very collected, and Baby hustling to stay beside him. Together, we laughed.

As the tide became lower, we had more space to play. *Ahhhh, this is the life.* I sighed.

As we played, having so much fun, my mind wandered back to when I was a girl and would go for long rides with friends and being silly, like Abby and I were then.

We continued to perform spirals, teardrops, yin yens, and circle chains, all the while like two kids instead of adult and teenager. For a little while, there was no age difference. We were friends, not instructor and student.

Lynn and Kara caught up, and we played a game of Tick Tack Toe in the sand. This turned out to be more difficult on horseback than we thought, and our mood became a lot more silly.

"This is *really fun,*" Kara giggled. By now we were all laughing hard.

King gave me a sudden buck telling me he needed more work. He was a high energy Arabian and needed *lots* of work to keep him sane. I galloped circles around the others as they played in the more gentle gaits. Follow the leader. Laughing at the mistakes they were making. The horses seemed to be having fun as well. We were moving back down the beach, towards the parking lot.

"Hey, Vicki, look!" Lynn noticed that there was a sand bar that looked like an island oasis. It was open, huge, and calling to us to venture over.

We wanted the girls to have the whole beach experience. We waded through the water. It was only inches deep. That little pond of water was trapped by sand all around and was very still. Because the water was not moving, Baby walked across like the trusty steed she usually was.

The sand bar was as big as a football field and was so inviting. Even better, we could see the seals in the cove just to our left. They were also trapped in their own little pond of water.

"Oh *wow!* Look at the baby one." Kara was transfixed on that black, shinny pup as it lay in the sun just basking in the lush warmth of it.

"Lets explore around the edge and see what we can see in the water." Lynn was in an exploratory mood. "Hey look! There is an old lobster trap."

"Be careful girls, do not get caught up in the ropes hanging off the lobster trap. Better to stay clear of it," I warned.

"Look at all the clams!" Abby exclaimed.

"You want to take some home?" I joked.

"Yuck, no I don't think so." She wrinkled up her nose.

The girls were having so much fun and laughing and of course Lynn and I were acting like kids, getting sillier still, playing, certainly *not* acting our ages.

Time was no object as we played and horsed around.

In our fun, we forgot to keep an eye on the tide.

"It seems like we are a long way from the beach." Kara suddenly noticed.

"Wasn't the sand bar bigger?" Abby replied.

Being relaxed, Baby had been sniffing at a clam she happened to notice. She lifted her head at the sound of Abby's voice.

I looked over the sea towards the beach. My stomach churned.

When we waded to the sand bar, the tide had been low. Now the tide was coming back in, made obvious by the growing water between our fantasy island, and the beach. We were a long way from the beach. The sand bar was getting smaller every minute.

Oh no! I thought, panic rising up into my chest. I rode to Lynn and pretended not to have heard the girls. *I am responsible for these girls and I've got to get them out of here, and fast.*

"Lynn," I calmly started, "Don't panic, but we have to get off the sandbar *now!*"

I had interrupted her private concentrated play, and she snapped her head up noticing my tone of voice. Her face went white as reality took over.

"Keep your cool and just start going across. Keep going no matter what." I shakily said. "I will gather the girls up and we will be right behind you." I was worried about Abby and Baby. The mare was so small that she might have to swim, and she didn't even like the waves.

I took a few deep breaths and yelled in what I hoped was a cheery voice to the girls. "OK, it is time to go back. Kara, follow Lynn, Abby next, and I will bring up butt detail. *"If Baby doesn't want to go because of the waves, I will swat her on the butt with my whip to keep her going,* I told myself.

Kara was getting a little worried as she started behind Lynn, "Wow, this is deep!"

"Just keep going." I told her.

"Abby, follow Boy and don't stop no matter what. We really need to get back to the beach."

Abby looked at me, saw what I hoped was a calm, smiling face, and went on to follow Kara and Boy. I brought up the rear with King.

As Baby started following Boy, she snorted at the waves. She began to back up. "Abby, swat her!" I said quickly.

Abby swatted her on the butt with the short crop. Baby bucked up, kicked out her hind leg, then decided she better go.

I was behind her with King. Baby once again questioned our decision. I kept King moving. He nudged her with his chest. This booted her forward!

The look in Baby's eye was *I don't like this one bit.* She had no choice. She was sandwiched between Boy and King.

I watched as Baby suddenly seemed to be floating. When a wave came in, pushing us all inland, her hooves were not touching the ground! I could see this clearly in the transparent water as she would flutter her legs.

Baby was indeed swimming! Her 13.2 hand frame wasn't tall enough to just wade through.

"This feels like riding in deep snow!" Abby reflected.

It may feel the same but is quite different. I thought.

"Abby, let her reins be really loose and let her handle it. Grab the top of her breast plate and sit as still as you possibly can. No peeking over the side."

I knew it would scare her if I told her the truth. Horses are very buoyant. Like a huge ball, they can easily be turned over. If she leaned forward or to the side it would be possible to drown Baby, and herself in the process.

Each wave that came in seemed to push us towards the beach and I was grateful for that. We finally made it! As we waded in toward safety, I was so tempted to get off and kiss the ground.

Poor Abby and Baby were totally soaked except for Baby's head and Abby's chest and head. Baby, bounding through the water, coupled with the waves pushing from behind, made them both get a, cold, salty bath.

Lynn escaped with just a little above her knees getting wet. Her horse being over 16 hands.

Boy and King being a little over 15 hands, had to struggle through the water, which was almost to the top of our saddles.

I said a silent thank you prayer to God, and my insides began to stop their flutters. I could see that Lynn was also still shaken. The Girls didn't seem to be bothered by it at all. Being young they didn't fully appreciate the danger we were in. Just another big adventure.

"Look how wet we are!" Kara remarked.

"Yeah , my boots are full." Abby added. They were more bothered by the fact that they were wet, and getting a little cold.

I lifted my leg and let the water drain out of my boots. "Hey look girls, can you do this?" I was trying to brighten the situation. The girls started laughing as they tried to imitate my action.

"Whoops, Abby be careful." I called to her as she almost fell off Baby. Baby didn't appreciate the sudden rush of water beside her, and had stepped sideways.

"What do you think girls, should we call it a day?" I suggest.

"Oh, can we stay for a little while longer, till we dry a little bit?" Abby begs.

"You girls aren't too cold?" I asked.

"Nope," they say in unison.

"Well...what do you think Lynn?" I questioned.

"Sure, why not," she answered.

"OK then. Lets go. We can trot and canter to warm up." I finalize.

As the air was very warm, over 50 degrees, with a warm breeze still blowing, we were drying fast so we played for about another half hour. We walked and talked and said "hellos" to people walking their dogs. We hated for the day to end.

A reporter from a local newspaper came around since it was an unusually warm day and took some pictures of the beach and people on it. He asked if we would mind if he took some of us to put in the paper. Of course we never mind having pictures taken of our horses and it would be a good memory of the day for the girls to have.

By now the beach was disappearing as the tide was almost completely in.

As we rode off the beach, I sneaked a look back at where our fantasy island *had been* and shuddered inwardly at what could have been.

We un-tacked the horses and as was our beach day custom, let them roll in the deep sand. It is so funny to watch King roll, flopping down before we can really get all the way down, get up only as far as his belly and then flop to the other side like a fish out of water, doing this repeatedly until he was satisfied. Then flinging himself up and giving a couple of huge bucks, just for fun. The others rolled in a more normal fashion, usually only once on each side.

Baby rolled once and then glared at the advancing waves, giving them her last evil eye warning. As we turned around to leave the beach, she gave a kick in the air towards those horrible waves, just for extra measure.

We packed up and on the way home went into our favorite cafe' that

had nice hot soup and sandwiches. For the hour and a half trip home we bought lattes for Lynn and me, hot cocoa for the girls and giant cookies for all. I could tell the girls were really beat and I know Lynn and I were. We were glad to be on the way home. I was ready to take a hot bath and relax.

HURTING AND HEALING

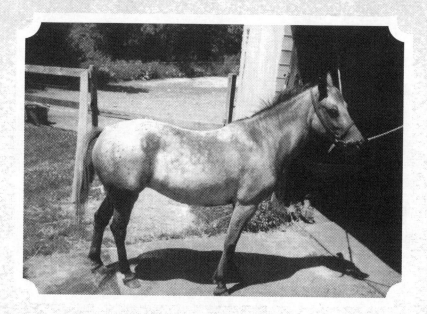

Baby, Thirteen..

When Baby was thirteen, she was in her prime; however, I had no one riding her. Abby had gone away to college, and the rest of my students were riding other horses. I didn't have time to work multiple horses for my personal use. But that didn't stop the fact that Baby needed and deserved attention and work. These factors contributed to a hard decision to sell Baby.

I sold Baby to a friend of mine, Sarah with the promise that she would get lots of work. I made a promise with Sarah that if she was no longer wanted Baby, I would buy Baby back for the same price I was paid.

All went well for that summer. Baby was doing well, and Sarah and her family seemed to enjoy her. Sarah had young nieces and nephews who loved riding Baby.

Then, once again, Baby wasn't being worked enough. Her feed did not get cut back to reflect her decrease in exercise. What does a pony do that isn't being worked and has food in front of her twenty four seven? She eats and gets fat.

I periodically visited Baby at her new home. Gradually, I saw her gaining weight. I worried about her health. I had never seen her this heavy before.

I mentioned this to Sarah as we leaned against the fence one afternoon watching Baby and her pasture mate. Baby's abdomen hung lower than her girth.

Sarah looked at me with hurt in her eyes as if I had told her something painful. Then she pursed her lips and crossed her arms. "She's not *that* overweight."

I had insulted Sarah. I didn't say anything more, but inside I felt anger and fear. Since Baby was no longer mine, I had no control of the situation.

Then the winter of Baby's second year there, Abby and I visited her at Christmas Time and to bring her carrots. Abby was home from college for the holidays, and was looking forward to seeing Baby.

I had warned Abby that Baby had gotten big, but to my dismay she was even fatter. She looked like a giant ball with legs. She had no visible back bone. I couldn't even see her withers. They just blended in with her back. From her ears to her tail there was a roll of fat on either side of where the spine would be. Her croup was just two huge lumps side by side.

"Oh, my God. Baby, how did you get so fat?" I started to tear up as I hugged her. I knew it was out of my hands. I felt helpless and actually felt panicked. I thought of all types of scenarios.

Was Baby fed too much grain? I didn't think that was likely as I had told Sarah exactly what I was feeding for grain, which was a scant handful, and I trusted that it hadn't increased. Was she out on grass all day? It was winter, so that wasn't possible. Could she have a condition like Cushing's or a problem with her thyroid? Those conditions take years to develop. Then how did she get so fat and so quickly? I agonized about it.

Abby and I left. Both of us were crying. I remember saying to Abby, as my heart was breaking, "I know she is going to founder, just wait and see. No horse can be that fat and not founder!"

April of 2004, Baby foundered. She was in her third week at the equine hospital when Sarah called me.

My friend, having dealt with two other foundered horses in the past , didn't want to deal with rehabilitation of another foundered pony.

"I'm going to put Baby to sleep," she told me.

I felt like I had been punched in the stomach. If only I could have done something to improve Baby's lifestyle. I shouldn't have even sold her. Now she was this ill and about to put down. I couldn't bare it.

"Let me buy back Baby!" I told Sarah suddenly.

She seemed started. "You want her back?"

Ron and I were in the process of moving. We really did not have the extra money to buy back Baby, but I couldn't bear to give up Baby. I borrowed the money.

We were staying with friends at their farm for about a month while we were readying our new place. I couldn't wait until we moved to get Baby. As soon as she was released from the equine hospital, I brought her to our friends' farm with our other horses where we were staying.

As soon as I had Baby settled into her new, temporary stall, I used an equine weight measurement tape to see how much she weighed.

She was over one thousand pounds!

And she had lost weight since the last time I had seen her. This was much too heavy for a 13.2 hand pony. Baby's normal weight was eight hundred pounds.

The tears and the anger I felt returned. But now I had Baby in my care again. I had full determination to get her well again.

And so it was the beginning of a new relationship between Baby and me. She was the patient and I was the nursemaid. I was planning on retiring from training and instructing. I didn't need to work. We only had two other horses so I had plenty of time to spend with her.

My farrier said it would take a total of three years to completely heal a horse that has foundered to the extent that she had. We were in for a long haul.

I spent a lot of money on her medications, special shoeing and a lot of time in her rehab. I put her on a diet of just a handful of grain to mix with her supplements and medications and one thin flake of hay three times a day. I had never been this strict with her but needed to bring her weight down fast. I had called the vets to see if she had been tested for Cushing's and thyroid problems. They said there was no indication that she had either problem. Just being that fat had caused her founder.

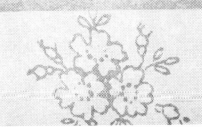

It was so hard to watch Baby as she devoured her hay in no time. She had become used to eating a lot more than that. I agonized along with her. I, too, love food, so could imagine if I got it doled out to me that I'd never feel like it was enough. She then would stand in her little paddock and watch the other horses eat, with the saddest eyes I ever saw.

I thought about this a lot and devised ways to make her hay last longer. I would shake and spread it all around her paddock so she had to move around to eat and find every sprig, which would simulate grazing. I also would give her the coarsest hay as that would force more chewing time. In this way it took her much longer to eat , and kept her moving around as well. I also kept a huge bucket of water in her paddock and she would play in it and drink more to feel fuller.

I spent many hours just grooming her, trimming her and taking her for long walks in hand, and I would let her have a mouthful of grass now and then.

We were forming a bond that formally had not been there. Before I had always been her handler and trainer. Now Baby relied on me in a different way. She was a new project to take up the time I would have formally been working. I was her new pal. Someone to spend a lot of time with. The only one who fed and pampered her.

When I felt that she could go for short rides, I once again simply hopped on bareback like during her very first rides behind Suzanne. I didn't bother with a bridle, just used her halter and lead. I rode her on quiet walking rides to help her heal.

She has not had any trouble with her weight again as I keep a close watch on her and don't let her get above eight hundred pounds. I prefer her weight to be about seven hundred and fifty but I do let it fluctuate

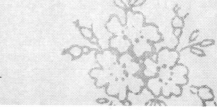

for winter warmth. Horses always loose weight in the spring due to losing the winter coat and using energy to put on a brand new summer coat, so letting them get a little fatter in winter isn't a bad thing.

Once we moved into our new place, I found that retiring from teaching wouldn't happen just yet. A few local people saw that I had horses and asked if they could ride. I knew that this was an opportunity for Baby to get worked lightly. All the students were beginners. Once again , Baby was to be a school horse.

Mae became a dedicated student who would ride her for the next six years. I had several handicapped kids ride her as well. Then a few of my friends that come to ride when they are in Maine, also still rode with me.

I rode Baby a lot myself getting her fit and healthy.

From her back, I thought about my plans for her and life in general. I always felt safe on Baby's back. It was easy and comfortable riding Baby, and our new connection made these moments special.

A DIFFERENT KIND OF WORK

APR 29 2006

With my unit 2006

I joined the Maine Equestrian Search and Rescue in the fall of 2004. I certified King in the next spring of 2005 and Baby in 2006 because it was recommended to have two certified horses per person in case one horse was unable to do a "call out".

To certify with the State of Maine, horses have to spend a weekend at a designated grounds where testing can be done.

On the first day, following check-in, riders and horses testing would all go on a trail ride to see how horses got along with each other on trail. On the ride, horses needed to cross or pass all obstacles provided. Baby

was usually ridden by me with a halter, and it was impressive to some of the testers. To me it was just how it was done with us.

After the trail ride, the horses had to load into *any* horse trailer. Amongst the group, we had a variety of trailers to test each horse. We had step-ups, three horse slant loads, one and two horse ramp loads, and open stock trailers. Baby excelled at this. She has always been willing to enter any trailer anywhere for anyone.

Overnight, horses had to be tethered between two trees without fussing. No problem for Baby. As long as there was food, she was happy to be tied anywhere.

The second day is the bulk of the testing. In the arena, the horses were ridden through all the gaits to see how obedient they were with a lot of commotion and other horses around. Most of us were either show riders, Endurance riders or both, so the horses were used to a lot of horses milling around. Then they had to stand for a few minutes without fussing. Most horses looked around. Baby lowered her head and took a snooze.

Then the dogs were let loose (just friendly family dogs who are used to horses). Some of the horses didn't like this much. Baby used to chase dogs out of her pasture because she was attacked by a Black Lab when she was just a filly. When I started riding her I had to train her *not* to chase dogs. Baby was fine now as we have always had dogs around our place. She learned that most dogs didn't chase her.

Next we each had to pony and be ponied (lead and be led) from another horse. These were things I did normally to exercise more than one horse on trail, so Baby was fine with this as well but didn't see the point

of it in the arena. She laid her ears back and kind of let herself be dragged around when she was being ponied but was much happier when it was her turn to lead a horse.

The next exercises demonstrated how the horse would behave if a rescued person needed to ride it out of the woods. Each horse had to be mounted and dismounted from both sides. It had to be ridden by another person and by a person who did not know how to ride. As a forgiving school horse that had been ridden by many new riders, Baby did excellent at this exercise.

Next kids rode bicycles in between and around the horses. Most were fine with that as well. Baby wanted to follow them.

Then came the raincoats! Usually I can put on and take off outer clothing like jackets, rain gear or ponchos while sitting in the saddle. For some reason that day she didn't like the huge yellow rain slicker we all had to put on and take off! In fact, none of the horses liked the tester bringing it to them, walking right up to their faces with the big, yellow, open rain slicker, flopping from his hand. Most of the horses wanted to leave the premises. *Fast!* Baby was at the front of that pack. Their reactions were funny, but understandable because usually the riders take a jacket out of their saddle bags to wear. We have never had someone actually come towards us with it like that.

Each horse got used to it and we all passed eventually. We kept repeating that lesson just to make sure. We passed the dreaded raincoat back and forth between us. We made a game of it, laughing the whole time. We would ride around the arena and suddenly pass it to someone. After a while the horses ignored this.

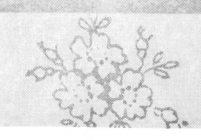

The testing up until then showed that horses were versatile. Now it was time to apply their versatility in a search and rescue scenario. The next exercise was the most important as it was a test course in the woods, and each horse and rider went alone. I pretended to search for a lost person.

I looked for signs of anyone having been there, noting aloud what I saw. The examiners were around to note my observations. They stood quietly out in the open off the trail and hid at obstacle. These obstacles included props set up in the woods, A-frame shelters, objects to step over, bridge to cross, things hanging from overhead that we had to go under, and a gun was fired when I least expected it.

Baby passed all this with flying colors.

That was until a terrified "hiker mom" came at us wearing a backpack, waving her arms and screaming, "My little boy is missing! Have you seen him? I cannot find him!"

This Baby did not like, and she tried to leave the woods. She quickly spun totally around, kicking out with both hind feet at the terrifying object coming at her. I couldn't help but laugh. This is typical of her when she truly is scared, not just being a brat pretending.

I was able to keep her in one place, but she still bucked and kicked! I made her stay until she calmed down. When I heard her chewing, relax and heave a huge sigh, I knew she was ready to face her attacker, I turned her around and let her know that it was truly just a person, not some monster. (huge protruding metal framed backpacks tend to look very strange to horses).

Since I was able to control her movements and she didn't leave all together, trusting me to tell her it was OK, she passed that test.

Then next time the screaming woman came around, Baby was much better with it, although she did still shrink down a bit.

The exercise finished as we came out of the woods to come back to camp. It was on the main road and the testers came around with cars and trucks to see how our horses were with traffic. If simple traffic was OK, they beeped the horn. Of course all the horses were fine with that.

We had just one more check to do. Do a grid search with another rider because in a real situation, we would always search in pairs. My partner and I rode through a large hilly field into the woods and back out again, looking for a lost hunter. A wallet, glove, boot print, hat, lighter and candy wrapper were placed for us to see. We had to remember what we saw.

Most of the teams were very observant and found them all. I found something extra not placed by our testers—a pair of underwear in a tree!

That part of the test was fun and not stressful at all. It was perfect ending to our day.

When I got my score card, I was pleased to find that Baby passed with high scores! She was a state certified search and rescue horse!

One time we were called out for a "search and recover," which meant that we were not likely to find the person alive, since she was "missing and presumed dead."

I lived the further away from the search site, and I picked up my partner, Jean, and her horse along the way. We continued on to the command post, some one hundred miles away, for our orders and map of where the Maine State Wardens wanted us to search.

It is not a very exciting place, this command post. All is very low keyed rather slow. I was expecting all kinds of noise and the sound of radios, like on TV. That wasn't the case. There were several command trailers and we had to find the one for Equine Search. There were tents with food and coffee enough to feed the army of searchers present that day.

Since we were a little later, the dog teams, four wheeler teams and foot teams, were already out searching. There were a few still waiting for their orders of where to search.

We had to find our dispatcher. Jean and I left the horses in the trailer munching hay. We went from one portable emergency trailer to another until we found the trailer where our dispatcher was. He took our badges. These would be returned when we returned. That is the best way to make sure everyone gets back and they don't have to have a search for the search and rescue. He gave us a map and explanation of where we were to go and where we were to stop. These were our orders.

Our teammates had gotten there earlier and been given their orders. They were already out.

We trailered out to the logging landing site where we parked the trailer. We unloaded the horses, tacked up, packed our food and water plus grain for the horses. We set our buckets of water out for later when the horses would need a drink and be sponged off. Then we headed out on the trail that was marked for us on the map.

We rode side by side along the logging road, looking over our own side of the trail. It was very slow work in the hot sun that day. Our search was to recover a body. I wanted to be successful with the mission, however, my heart went out to the victim, and I hoped that the evidence was wrong, that she wasn't dead.

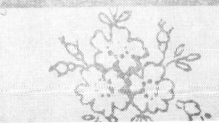

Two hours went by. We saw many trash sites with garbage bags, old tires and stained mattresses, but nothing that seemed suspicious. Then something caught my eye.

"Look, Jean!" I pointed. "What do you suppose is in that tarp?" I had site of a tarp down in the ditch, almost hidden, covering what looked like something human shaped. "Radio in and see if I have the authority to look inside, would you please?"

Jean carried the radio and made contact with our command officer. She described the tarp to him.

"Open it and tell me what you see," he instructed. "I'll stay on the radio. Over."

"Do you want the honors?" Jean asked as we looked at each other.

"Sure. No problem." I replied. I got off Baby and handed her reins to Jean. I walked down in the ditch. "OK, here goes!"

I gingerly rolled the tarp covered item to find an opening. It was heavy. Like a body? I found a loose corner to lift. I took a deep breath and readied myself for a gruesome sight and putrid smell of...

Someone's old Christmas tree!

"Oh, my goodness," I began. "I just can't believe it."

"What do you see?" Jean asked tentatively. "Wait one second. Over," I heard her say to command.

"Why would anyone throw a fully decorated Christmas tree away in a tarp, and way out here? This is beyond bizarre," I said disgustedly. I was relieved as well as disappointed. No one *wants* to find a dead body but we wanted to be able to give the family closure. And that was our job.

Jean reported to the waiting officer what we have found. Laughter on the other end told us they found this funny.

We laughed about that as well. I got back on and we moved on up the trail.

At about noon we were radioed and asked if we wanted lunch brought out to our site. We said thank you but we brought our own with us. They are always amazed that Equine Search and Rescue is self-sufficient.

As Equine Search and Rescue, we always brought something to eat and drink. Our horses drank ground water and ate water laden grass, and we carried grain and carrots as well. We were trained to stay out for as long as forty-eight hours without help.

At about four o'clock, we were radioed to return. The search was over for the day. There were no results on anyone's try. They had six Equine teams, several Canine teams, two four wheeler teams, and untold foot searchers. We all together covered about 50 miles of Maine woods with no results at all. I wished we could have brought closure for the victim's family.

The Search and Rescue experience was a very valuable time in my life. It brought Baby and I so much closer. I got training that I would never have otherwise had. Every month we would have a meeting. Mounted when the weather would allow. Unmounted when inclement.

I feel I made some very special friends within my unit, and even not am in contact with several.

I believe it is still the only Equine Unit in the State of Maine. If time would allow, I would still be involved in it.

BACK IN THE SADDLE

"Ouch! What are you doing?" I yelled at the person poking me.

Why have I got sand in my mouth and eyes? I can't see! Where is King? What are these people saying? Who are these people? Where am I? What is going on? Who is talking? Why am I being lifted up?

These thoughts ran through my mind at lightning speed. I was very confused.

"I am trying to put in an IV. Hold still." the medic said as he sighed.

"Well, can't you do it without it hurting so much?" I complained. "I give blood and it doesn't hurt this much!"

"If you hold still it won't hurt so much," he cautioned.

"What happened? Where is King? What is going on? I need to finish my ride."

"You have had an accident. We are taking you to the hospital. You are in an ambulance," he told me calmly. "Your horse is fine. He has been taken to the checkpoint,to be checked out by the vet and where your husband is waiting with the trailer. There will be no more riding for you today." The medic answered each question.

I remember asking several times where King was. Otherwise I don't remember anything else except waking up in the hospital with Ron by my side.

I had three broken ribs, fractured left shoulder, concussion and contusion on my brain, torn meniscus in my left knee, and a sprained right hip.

"I want to go home," I told the doctor.

"You can go home when you can walk up and down the stairs with the help of your husband. But not until tomorrow," he informed me with a stern voice. "Tonight you stay in the hospital for observation on your head injuries."

I woke up the next day, and as soon as my husband was there, I asked for the nurse to take me to where I can go up and down stairs so I could go home.

She took us to the therapy room where there was a set of three stairs. Ron and I walked up and down it with hesitant steps several times until the nurse was satisfied.

Then she handed me a cane and said, "Now walk up and down with this, and I will talk to the doctor about you going home."

I did it with difficulty, but I did it!

I went home in the afternoon. Ron helped me into the barn where I could check on King. He ignored me as he continued to eat his hay.

"The vet said he was fine. Not even a scratch." Said Ron.

"Phew, I was so worried about him," I said with tears in my eyes.

I looked at my helmet. It had a perfect hoof shaped dent in it. I cringed at the sight of that. I imagined what my head would look like if I had not been wearing the helmet.

I then went into the house. It was rest for me (the doctor said for at least eight weeks if not ten). He also said that there would be no riding for at least three months for my head to heal (dizziness to go away) and

my shoulder to heal. I may have to have surgery on my knee. My shoulder, ribs and hip would heal on their own.

Later, my riding companions filled me on their perspective of my accident. King looked like his hind end was picked up and flung over his head, with me ending up under him. In struggling to get up, he stepped on my head and drove it into the sand. The rider closest to me told me of the awful gurgling noises I made while I was out. I remember nothing!

I am not the sort of person that can simply sit and do nothing but watch TV. I was expected to do just that! I was not to move any more than necessary. I breathed into the breathing apparatus several times a day so I wouldn't get pneumonia from taking too shallow a breath because of the broken ribs. I slept on a wedge pillow as I could not breathe lying flat, and my shoulder would not let me sleep flat either. I walked with a cane when I had to walk, but otherwise I was "not supposed to move."

I was bored, itching to do my own chores and to ride. I could not stand this. After a week, I snuck into the barn and one handedly picked out the stalls with my little trailer super fork. Ron came home and gave me a talking to about it. I did it anyway, every day.

After a month, I made up my mind to ride against my doctor's orders. Yes, I am a stubborn person. My horses mean a lot to me and are my life. And darn it, I wanted to ride!

I turned to Baby for my first ride. I wanted to ride so badly, but knew that King's bouncy gaits and unpredictable actions were not going to be tolerable yet.

I invited Heather and another friend to come for a "lazy trail" ride. I also lured them with a cookout afterwards.

"Since this is my first ride after my accident, it will be very slow, and if it hurts too much, we will come back early. Is that OK with you girls?"

Heather said, "Yes I am ready for a slow ride. I hurt my knee during the ride last month when Mariah fell into a mud hole."

I got Baby ready. I climbed on the mounting block. I knew that even though she was short, my knee wasn't working well enough to just get on from the ground. My hip was also still very sore. And my shoulder wasn't healed either. Probably my ribs were not either, but I knew she would not pull on my arms.

We left the yard and rode through the trail across the street from my house. It was an old railroad bed and followed the river.

"Oh, this is wonderful!" I said. "I have missed this trail so much. I have missed riding so much."

Both of my companions agreed it was beautiful on this trail.

We crossed the road to get onto another trail. It also was discontinued railroad bed and was smooth and inviting.

"Let's try trotting a little. OK with you two?" I asked.

"Sounds good," they agreed.

We trotted a little and it didn't hurt. I tired easily, so after a mile, I walked again.

"That felt good, but, boy, am I tired." I was breathing rather heavily, which I could not believe. Just a month ago, I was in good enough shape to ride a hundred miles.

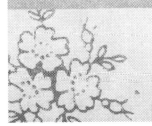

"You know that injuries and healing takes a lot out of a body." Heather said.

"I guess so. I feel so weak. I just can't believe it," I replied. I had planned about a twelve mile ride. "Do you girls mind if we take the short cut back? I am really wobbly and tired. Or you can finish the loop if you want to." I thought I was beginning to whine.

Neither girl minded the early termination. Our ride would be only about eight miles by the time we rode back into the yard.

When we returned, the girls put their horses in paddocks for the rest of the day. Ron cooked on the grill. Both my friends had brought a pot luck dish to share. I had a huge salad to share as well and s'mores for after. We had a really nice relaxed visit.

It didn't take long for me to fall asleep that night!

I rode Baby for the next month. Usually my little woods trail, no more than an hour and a half. Then when I thought I had healed, and with the doctor's blessing, I eagerly took King for my first ride on him since our accident.

Although I had always been able to ride him with no problem, his antics and jumping around now hurt me, something I hadn't considered before getting in his saddle. I had always been able to ride him and laugh about his silliness. I was not laughing any more. I was dreading every ride on him, knowing that my body wasn't going to handle it well anymore.

Over the next few months, I found myself riding Baby more and more and King less and less. It always hurt after riding him, and it didn't seem to get better. He liked to do "airs above the ground" and to yank me

back and forth like a rag doll constantly. My body had just had too much trauma to be able to sit it out any more. I still wanted to compete in Competitive Trail and Endurance but knew I could not do it on King.

I decided to try Baby at it. She had taken a few of my students on competition but never me. Although I was sad about my decision to stop competing on King, I would have a new experience to ride Baby competitively. I was excited.

WATER WATER EVERYWHERE

Arcadia 50 CTR 2006

It was raining heavily when I fed Baby her breakfast on day one of Acadia 50 Competitive Trail Ride.

"Boy, how did you like that rain last night?" I asked a fellow competitor who was feeding her horse in the stall beside me.

"Wasn't that something?" She said. "It rocked our camper with all that wind." she continued.

"I am so glad we get to have stalls here. It seems like a luxury not to have paddocks and tents in this weather." I say gratefully.

The rain let up briefly as we tacked up, but came back as the timer sent out the first riders. Baby and I stayed in the barn to stay dry, while riders went out in twos, two minutes apart. I was going last as I had offered to pull down markers for the ride manager. Also that way if I was going slow it would be OK. I wouldn't be holding anyone else up. If I needed to pull from the ride I could still remove the markers in my own sweet time.

The rain was very cold for this time of year. Felt icy even. Our horses wore polar fleece or wool rump covers to keep their large rump muscles from getting chilled. I wore my Gore-Tex military raincoat, a gift from my Army son. I was grateful I had the foresight to take it along. It was big enough to cover the top of my thighs and the hood fit over my helmet. The arms were long enough to cover my hands in the pelting rain. I was toasty warm underneath it.

I walked Baby back and forth in the isle while I waited for the last rider to leave. Baby was patient. She never worried about being left behind. She had always been really good about that.

As the last rider was trotting off, I led Baby outside, mounted and warmed her up at the trot in a circle. Five minutes passed then the timer said, "You are good to go. Have a great ride."

"Thank you." I said as I trotted past her. "See you at the check point."

We started up the trail in a nice swinging trot. I was surprised by how much water was pouring off the rock wall on my left. Baby noticed this as well! She decided she didn't like the rushing waterfall and went as

close to the right edge of the trail as she could. A few widely spaced boulders was all there was to stop us from tumbling down the mountainside in this national park.

I saw a potential disaster, and gave her a hard kick to get her attention. I pulled her to the left, back towards the waterfall from above.

My accident with King was still fresh in my mind, and I didn't want another one. My heart was pounding as I looked down hundreds of feet to the rocks below.

Baby, finally realizing that we are not going back, scrunched down, as if it was going to fall on her, and rushed by, head and tail high and snorting loudly.

"OK, Baby. It is all right," I said to her breathlessly. When she realized it wasn't following, she slowed to the nice working trot that I had planned.

There were several places such as this where the rocks above had formed waterfalls. Baby finally got used to it. With a little hesitation she rushed by each one.

These carriage roads were the best footing, solid, not slippery, in the wet weather, though they were steep in some places. The stone bridges were solid and railed, and arched. The view was so beautiful as we crossed them. There was a whole forest of pine trees and leafy cedars below us with a narrow road down the middle. Chipmunks scurried along the sides down below. Squirrels peeked out from behind trees as we came off the bridges into the forest once again.

The markers I pulled down were on the signposts. I sidled Baby over to each one as we came upon them pulled the small, plastic arrows down, staples and all, being careful to pull only "day one" markers. I then put them into the bag that I had brought hanging from my breast plate for this purpose.

At the half way point, we cantered into the hold. Baby passed the vetting, and a half-hour later, we were once again on our way up the next beautiful carriage trail.

Baby and I felt very good. It was still rainy but getting muggy. I shed my raincoat and passed it to one of the spotters along the trail. I would have been just as wet from sweat as I would be from the rain, I figured. At least I would be cooler. This rain was much more comfortable. It was very good for keeping Baby cool. As I pulled off more markers, Baby got to eat grass each time, just a mouthful or two, but it added up, and she was doing great.

Day two went much like day one on the same trails and with the same schedule, however, the weather was better. It was still cloudy, but it rained little. We were all grateful for that. Everything was damp and sticky.

Baby and I passed the finish line in plenty of time even though we were slowed down marker pulling. Baby got a score of 96 out of 100. Not bad for a 50 mile CTR. It was a great weekend.

I was so proud of Baby for taking me on my first competition after my accident. I also could relax now that I knew she could handle my weight with no problems at all on a ride. Fifty miles on steep hills is not easy and carrying almost a quarter of her weight made it even more incredible. It felt so good to be competing again and felt so comfortable to be doing it on Baby. I always felt relaxed on her. She not only took care of herself, but me too.

MUD SPA

Pine Tree 50 Endurance ride 2006...
used by permission of Kate Rogers..

Three thirty on a balmy Saturday morning, I woke up to the alarm on my watch. Time to get up, feed Baby and myself. We would be headed out on trail at five o'clock sharp! This would be the Pine Tree 50/100 Mile Endurance Race. I had chosen the fifty mile distance.

I sat up, took a deep breath, looked around at the many other trailers and trucks in the fairground field. I opened the truck door (the air outside wasn't much cooler than inside the truck) and slid out of the reclined seat.

I walked slowly to the fairground bathroom to splash cold water on my face to wake me.

Back at the campsite, I started making noises as I prepared Baby's food. There were several nickers close by from horses whose owners have yet to arise. All horses know the sound of grain being prepared and all are suddenly very hungry.

I gave Baby her food and stumbled to the "snack shack" for my first cup of coffee and to see what might be there for breakfast that I wanted to eat. Donuts are the usual morning fare at rides in Maine (which feels like I have eaten a lead ball) so I bring my own breakfast food most of the time. That day there was oatmeal in little packets and hot water in a coffee pot. I made myself a bowl of oatmeal. I knew I would need the energy later. I spotted peanut butter and added a blob for the protein. I poured a cup of coffee and headed back to the barn with my breakfast.

By then, Baby had eaten her grain mixed with carrots, apples, electrolytes, soaked beet pulp along with her regular supplements. She has had hay in front of her all night, so she is ready to be groomed.

I gave her a thorough grooming, picked out her feet and checked her shoes to make sure they were secure for the fifty miles we were to go that day. I tacked her up, making sure that the saddle pad had no wrinkles to irritate her tender skin and that the girth wasn't too tight and she could breathe freely.

All my saddle packs were full of emergency items. I also carried GU, an energy packet for me, along with electrolytes for Baby, and a host of other items I might need or that might be needed by someone else. I carried a lot of supplies with me on rides so that I would be prepared to handle any situation.

Baby was ready.

Ron, my husband , who had just arrived at the grounds, came over and gave me a good morning kiss. "Hi, sweetie," he said to me. "Did you sleep OK?"

"I did. Slept like a rock." I replied.

I handed Baby to him and went into the back of the trailer to get changed into my tights and tee shirt. "She can eat grass while I get ready," I told him. "Be careful, she is grumpy."

"OK, ma'am," he said with a crooked grin. "So what else is new?"

Ron knew how picky I was about how my horses were taken care of, especially at rides, and he indulged me. He also knew to be wary of *Big Butt Grumpy Piggy Baby.* She had been known to bite or kick when grumpy, not often but still – she is a mare.

"Have you got everything you need?" Ron asked as I walked back to retrieve Baby.

"Yeah, I think so," I said, thinking very hard. I hated to forget something.

"Are you sure?" Ron was always watching my back, trying to make sure I wasn't left wanting anything on these rides. He knew how important they were to me. This was my fun.

Ron was not only my husband, but pit crew extraordinary. He always came to the rides to make sure I had everything I'd need for the ride and everything packed in my vet check trunk.

I got on Baby and started riding down to the warm up near the trail head. I was keeping a watch on the time because I usually go back up to hide behind a building while the gun is fired and wait as most of the "hot shot" riders barrel away in a burst of speed.

I flexed Baby a little, rode some small circles, leg yielded, did a little shoulder in and haunches in to warm up her muscles and limber her. It would be a long ride, and I wanted to make sure she was well "oiled" for it.

That day my watch must have been slow because the gun went off while I was still warming up close to the starting line. I had no choice but to go along as we were on the front line at the moment.

We started out well. Baby acted like it was an everyday ride. She was always so level headed. We trotted up the pine tree lined country dirt road at a nice easy trot with about 40 other horses performing various gaits and tricks. We pulled over to the right and let all those who chose to go faster pass.

A few riders decided to turn back, not willing to go out with the rowdy group. They would wait until the pack got a couple miles ahead before starting their ride. Some of those riders were rookies, and others had young horses on their first Endurance ride.

Some riders were going one hundred miles that day and were in a hurry to get a good start. The rest, like me, had only planned on the fifty mile ride.

Baby stopped to take a drink from the little stream that flowed down the ditch on the side of the road and more riders passed us. She didn't care. She finished and then picked up her trot in a mannerly fashion. I kept thinking, *she is such a good pony, I am so glad I brought her. I can relax on Baby.* I settled in for a nice relaxed ride.

We continued up the three mile, steep dirt road that began the journey of our ride. At the double ribbon, a signal for a turn, we turned left to go into a heavily wooded trail with green moss and rocks to pick our way around. This was barely a foot path and we loved it! Birds were singing by now, and the air

is getting heavy, promising to be a very humid and hot ride. Baby and I didn't care. We both loved the heat.

Soon we were out on the next part of our ride where once again it was dirt road. We came to our first vet check at about fifteen miles into the ride. Ron met me at the check-in. I grabbed my in slip, put it into my card pack. I handed Baby to him so I could go to the porta pottie. He un-tacked and sponged her down to cool her.

When I got back, I took her, my ride card, time slip and waited for our turn in line at the vet check area. Ron continued to sponge Baby to make sure she would be perfectly cooled and normal. When it was our turn—

"Good morning, Art," I said to the vet waiting for me. I knew most of the vets by name and they know me. I had been on many rides before, but with other horses.

"Good morning, Vicki. How are you doing today? Ride going OK?" he asked me.

"Yeah, great. She is always such a good pony for me."

"EDPP?" He asked. He meant, was she eating, drinking, peeing and pooping. When I had first started competing in long distance, I thought they were just joking about that. Now I knew they were very serious. If a horse stopped doing *any* of those things, it was cause for alarm. It meant that the horse was not normal and could be in danger.

"She sure is. This is Baby we are talking about. She takes very good care of herself," I replied.

He took her pulse and respiration, felt her legs and tack area for swelling or soreness. There was none. "She looks great so far," he said. "Would you trot her down to the cone and back, please?"

I trotted her down the tar road for them to watch her for lameness. The vet took pulse and respiration again to make sure it hasn't spiked with that little trot out.

"Everything looks great! I wish all of them looked this good. You are good to go," the vet said.

"Thank you! See you on the next round." I waved.

Baby got all As, a high score, and we were cleared to go when our mandatory time was up.

This was when I looked around and saw that several of the leading riders had been pulled from the ride. They had gone too fast too soon, and their horses suffered for it. It was much too humid to go that fast. The heat index was dangerously rising.

Ron took Baby back to let her eat the grain mash that he prepared for her while I rested in the chair he brought for me, ate and planned the next part of the ride.

"I think we can go a little faster now." I said between bites of my granola bar. "She is doing great and so am I."

"Time to get ready to go," Ron said to me.

I looked at my watch. "Oh I guess it is!" I had relaxed a little too long and I was a little behind.

Ron held Baby while I got her tacked up to go. Baby was offered another drink of water and a bite of food. She accepted. After all she was a piglet. She was ready. I was ready.

It was about thirty miles into the ride as we neared the second vet check when we came to a deep, inviting puddle across the whole trail. I could see that some had opted to go around and into the woods, but many footprints had gone all the way through. Since Baby loved to drink from dirty puddles and there are a lot of natural electrolytes in muddy water, we continued on through.

Baby took a couple of steps in and took a drink. She took a few more steps in--

Suddenly we both disappeared into the water!

Baby came up floundering, lurching, and lunged further into it before leaping out the other side. Water spewed out her nostrils!

I was half on and half off over her head with all this unexpected and sudden movement. I coughed and sputtered.

She stood there and shook off what she could of the muddy water, almost shaking me off as well. I got off to check her over. We were both covered in mud but otherwise seemed OK. There was mud in my mouth, mud in my ears, mud in my pants (how?), mud in my boots squishing around.

Baby was no different color which was amazing. She was Appaloosa colored with a lot of brown. She too has mud in her ears and eyes.

"Oh my goodness, Baby!" I crooned. "What was that?"

I checked her shoes and they are tight so I mounted. Baby walked fine. I asked for a trot. Still fine, so we continued on to the vet check.

We got some funny looks as we took our "in time" slip, and Ron said, "Did you visit a mud spa while you were out there?" He was always such a comedian. I explained what had happened. Then went to tell the ride manager to warn other riders during the first vet check about the hole on the second loop. He said that no one else so far had any problems there.

"I did mark for riders to go around it so there would be no problems."

"Oh, I guess I didn't pay attention to that." I said meekly, as I felt a little chastised.

"The snowmobiler club put logs across the slush during the winter so the sleds wouldn't get ruined in the hole," he explained further.

Baby must have slipped on one and gone down. Other riders had made it through just fine. Or so I thought.

Before the day is out two other riders had the same experience as Baby and me.

One of them, my friend Heather, lost a stirrup off her saddle completely in that hole, and had to find a replacement for the rest of the ride. All others had no problems at all.

We got cleaned up; luckily it was a really hot day so the cold washing actually felt good to Baby and me. We took a little extra time for this and then vetted out fine and dandy to continue the ride.

Baby and I had been keeping a steady slow pace. "To finish is to win" was a good motto to follow when riding Endurance. I was not out there to race.

Leaving the second hold, as we rode on the power line, another puddle took off Baby's left front shoe.

"Well, Baby. Seems we are having a time of it," I said to her. "I guess we better go back and see if the farrier is still at the hold." I got off and retrieved the shoe. I doubted very much that the farrier would have such a small shoe with him, and I didn't think to bring an extra one with me. Having a shoe come off was rare for Baby.

I turned her around and headed back to the vet check hold. I was only about three miles out, so it wouldn't hold us up too much. Since we were in the middle of the pack by then, there would be plenty of horses still to vet.

I trotted in to the startled looks of those who thought I came in the wrong way. I spotted the farrier.

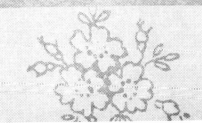

"Thank God he is still here, Baby," I said to her as I flew off her and ran to the farrier.

"Do you have time to straighten this shoe and put it back on my horse?" I ask hurriedly.

"Sure, you just caught me in between other horses." He smiled dollar signs.

He fixed and put on Baby's shoe. I told him my name so he could look me up back at camp after the ride for me to pay him.

I once again let management know I have left so they would not look for me, thinking I was lost.

Two more vet checks and no more strange happenings.

We finished in the middle of the pack with a score card to be proud of. Our ending vet scores were seven As, three B+s, and four B's. Very good scores for a fifty mile Endurance ride on such a hot and humid day. Baby got a week off from all work, a day for each ten miles of competition plus a couple extra..

"Despite our mishaps on that ride, it was one of my favorite competitions. Riding Baby was pleasurable and relaxing. I was comfortable riding her and appreciated her sane approach. With such a wonderful ride, I couldn't help but wonder what it would have been like if Baby hadn't been diagnosed with juvenile arthritis when she was a five-year-old. As much as I loved having Smokey and King as my competition horses, there was something comfortable and right about seeing the trail ahead between Baby's ears."

RACE AGAINST TIME

Hot Toddy 50 Endurance 2006

"Go! Go! Go!" The vets both yelled for me and Baby to gallop down the driveway and out to the trail. We only had a little over a half hour to finish the last ten miles of the fifty mile Endurance ride.

I entered the Hot Toddy Hustle at the last minute. I asked to pull ribbons for the ride manager in exchange for the entry fee. Since she needed to pull them down anyway, and it would be a lot of work, it sounded like a good deal to her as well as to me.

Baby and I arrived Friday afternoon. I set up a small, electric portable corral for Baby in the field with the gate opening at the bottom of the trailer ramp. I put one of the five gallon pails of water in the pen. All ready for the little princess, I unloaded Baby and set her free to eat grass.

"That's not going to last you very long, Baby, but will keep you busy for a little while," I said to her as she was chowing down.

I cleaned out the trailer and set up my cot. That was where I would sleep, and I could keep an eye on Baby. I swung open the divider and hooked it back, put Baby's tack on it ready for the next day, and set out my riding clothes.

It wasn't quite time to vet in, so I got my book and battery run boom box-CD player and relaxed on the cot with a snack of nuts and a bottle of water. I was happy for some quiet time. Later there will be plenty of people to talk to and say hi, but for now I just wanted peace.

An hour later I took the trek to the manager's tent to check-in, get my paperwork, food tickets and to find out what time the vetting would begin. Vetting would start soon, and would be in the indoor arena, I was told.

Back at the trailer, I ran a brush over Baby's already very clean coat. I picked out her hooves, making sure there are no little stones caught in her shoes that could cause her to move funny or step like something hurt.

I always liked to present a clean horse to the vets. They have to run their hands all over the horse to check it out, and I liked to have them at least not have to wash after handling my horse. It made me proud when they commented on how clean my horse was.

"Hi Heather." I spotted my friend Heather who is also riding. She saw me, too, and came over to chat.

There were many familiar faces that day, and more came over to where Heather and I were. We all stood and chatted, catching up on the Endurance gossip while waiting for our turn to be vetted.

Finally my turn. I had a dressage whip with me in case Baby didn't want to trot well. If I carried one at the beginning, the vets would not take points off if I also carried it at the end for the final vetting.

"Hello, Vicki." Art, the vet greeted me. "You are riding Baby tomorrow?" He asked.

"Yes, I am." I confirmed as he looked her over. Baby gave him a dirty look. I snapped her halter to let her know this would not be tolerated. She stood for him, knowing she will get a crack if she didn't.

"I see she is as grumpy as ever." He snickered.

"Yeah, I would think there was something wrong if she wasn't." I snickered right back.

"Looks good. Go ahead and trot her for me. You know the drill." Both vets were familiar to me and they also know Baby.

"Baby, ready? Taaarrottt." Baby, head at my shoulder, with ears laid back, jumps to start and begins to trot her little short, *I don't want to do this*, trot. I swung the whip behind me and slapped her belly with it. Her ears flipped forward, she jumped, and then trotted properly beside me.

At the cone, I let out the lunge line for her to circle around me to the left. I kept trotting in a smaller circle to keep her animated. "Brrrrrrr hoah," I said to get her attention. "Change," I commanded. She swung in toward me in a half circle and changed direction to trot at the end of the lunge in the opposite direction. I said "Brrrrrrr hoah" again to get her attention as I reeled her in by looping the lunge line. We continued to trot back to the vets in a straight line.

"She looks good. See you on trail," The head vet said to me.

"Thank you," I replied. "See you tomorrow."

I hung around with other riders I knew and chatted for a while as more of the competitors got vetted. Baby ate grass, happy as a clam. After a little while, I decided to head back to my trailer. Heather invited me to her trailer to hang out with her and some of the other riders. I thanked her anyway, but I wanted to enjoy some quiet time.

I meandered back to the trailer, letting Baby munch on the way back. I had parked at the end of the field so we could have not only a quiet place but also privacy.

I put Baby back in her paddock. She walked over to her water bucket and took a long drink and then to the corner by the ramp where she watched me recline on the bunk.

I reached over and turned on the boom box and put in my CD to listen to *Experiencing God*. I put my hands behind my head on top of the pillow. It was very restful, and I found myself singing along softly.

I watched as Baby dropped her head. Her lower lip started to twitch and hang. Her eyelids drooped, half closing. Her ears were flopped out to the side. She dropped one hip, toe down. As she relaxed, she sighed and began to snooze. She was totally relaxed and knew that we are safe. We had each other for company.

I woke up to Baby's soft nicker.

She would like her dinner, thank you very much!

"Wow I guess I was tired Baby. I am sorry," I said to her as I jumped up and looked at my watch. I began fixing her dinner of soaked beet pulp, grain, electrolytes, carrots and apples. I put it into her serving bowl,

which she gratefully accepted. Then I threw a couple flakes of hay in there for her as well. With the amount of grass still in the paddock she would probably not eat much of it, but it would be available if she wanted it. I topped off her water bucket.

The entry fee would take care of tomorrow's breakfast, snacks and dinner, but for tonight we were to fend for ourselves. For supper I had Greek yogurt, canned juice, and a turkey sandwich on whole grain bread. In the cooler I had several bottles of water. I also had nuts, granola bars and GU, which would go in my saddle bag during the ride in case I was hungry on trail. I would also have two prepared syringes of electrolytes for Baby.

"Early to bed Baby," I said after I ate my supper. I was ready to settle in for the night.

The last thing I remembered was the sound of the crickets and Baby as she was munching the hay I had given her. I was mildly surprised that she would eat hay instead of the still present grass.

Once again, I woke to Baby's soft nicker. She wanted her morning grain, or maybe she wanted company. But it was only 3:00, and I didn't have to be up until 4:30...plus it was cold that morning.

"Oh, Baby. Why do you have to eat right now?" I groaned.

She nickered again, nodding her head up and down and pawing. Baby is a very insistent horse.

"OK, OK." I rolled over. "I will get it."

I got up and gave Baby her grain mix, checked her water, and threw a couple flakes of hay to her. I then climbed back into the warm cot and went back to sleep.

My alarm went off and I got up for real. I checked to make sure Baby is all set and stumbled to the indoor ring for coffee and breakfast. Donuts were offered. *I should forgot the donuts and eat a granola bar,* I thought. *But a donut sure would taste good,* was my next thought.

My second thought won. I had a chocolate glazed donut and coffee. As I sat on a bale of hay that was put there for seating, I saw other competitors arrive and also get coffee and donuts.

"Good morning," I said to whomever walked in.

"Well, it is morning anyway. I don't know about good yet," was one reply I didn't expect. I was a morning person so those that were grumpy in the morning always took me by surprise.

Heather walked in, got her donut and coffee, and sat beside me. She, too, was not a morning person, but she knew I was and began to talk about her riding plan for the day.

"I will have to wait until all have gone through and be at the very end," I said. "Since I am pulling ribbons, I cannot pull them until all the competitors have been through the trail."

"That could make you late," Heather warned, "especially if someone decides to pull and doesn't care when they get in." She was always practical and reminded me of the fact that I *could* get eliminated for going over time.

"Oh, you are right. I didn't think of that when I told her I would pull markers. Oh man. I hope that doesn't happen."

By then, I was through my donut. Boy was it heavy in my stomach. But boy was it good!

"Well, see you on trail. Maybe," I said to Heather.

"Hope so," she replied as I walked over to throw away my paper cup.

We parted and went to get ready.

I hooked Baby to the side of the trailer, groomed her, and tacked her up. I left her tied because she might otherwise roll, saddle and all. That would not be good. I got myself dressed, packed my saddle bags, and made sure none of the tack is going to irritate Baby's tender skin.

Ron was not coming to pit for me at this ride. I expected it to be slow going, and the weather was cool. I wouldn't have any problems taking care of me and Baby.

I heard riders beginning to warm up their horses. I hopped on Baby, and we, too, went down to the starting line to warm up. I chose to warm up in the outdoor ring because few were in there as most were warming up in the field.

I worked on limbering Baby with Dressage movements. A little leg yielding, low flexing of the neck and head, walk, trot and canter circles, and various loops and changing direction constantly.

Since I was riding her in a halter with reins, I got a lot of funny looks. Most are riding in various harsh hackamores, bits, tie downs, martingales, and sliding reins. Baby was easy to handle, so we could be very comfortable.

The starter's gun went off. I waited in the arena until all the riders had gone. I followed the last of the fifty-milers. Some were doing thirty miles, and the trail was different, so I had to be sure that I was taking down the correct ribbons. I had a map but hoped I didn't have to use it.

All went well until we came upon a rider whose horse would only go if someone was in front of it. He was a huge Standardbred who needed company. His companion had to go on ahead and his owner thought he would be all right following whoever came along. The riders that came along just rushed on ahead, and he was baffled and wouldn't go past a walk.

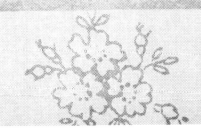

"I have to stay behind anyway so let me lead and he can follow," I said to her.

"That would be so nice," she said. "I just want to get to the first vet check, then I am going to pull. This is just too hard for him without his partner, and I don't want my husband to have to forfeit his ride for me."

So we continued in this fashion until the first vet check. She did pull and since she was the last, I was able to continue.

Pulling the ribbons was not as easy as I thought it was going to be. Usually the frail plastic ribbons were tied on and I could simply *pull* them off. These had all been put on with clothes pins and had to be unclipped to remove them. They also took up a lot of space so that the bag I usually used to pull ribbons filled way too quickly. I found myself getting creative finding places to put these clipped ribbons. I had them lined up on both sides of Baby's breast plate, clipped to her short mane, and even clipped to my riding tights.

"Here, take these please," I said to the spotters all along the way, as I took time to unclip and and hand those as well as the bagged ribbons to whomever was on the side of the road. There were a lot of spotters counting to make sure we all passed through. They knew that once they saw me, everyone had gone through or had been pulled.

I found as I went along that I was losing time. It was canter, stop, un-clip, canter, stop, un-clip the whole way.

It was a little cool, and there were showers throughout the day. That was very good for Baby as she was working harder than usual cantering and stopping constantly.

Despite the change in pace, Baby was in great shape at all vet checks, but I was alone at each check with one vet staying behind just for me. At the check points to make sure everyone got through, I was totally alone

with one person checking me off and telling me how far behind I was. All of the horses ahead of me had been vetted, stayed the mandatory half hour, and continued on with the ride. I was getting so very far behind because I had to stop and un-clip all those ribbons instead of simply riding by and pulling as I went like I had done many times before on other rides.

We finally got to the last check hold which was back at the farm. I felt a little lonely as I looked around at the bare fields. The food tent was already being taken down.

Most Endurance riders finish a fifty miler in 4-6 hours. I had by now taken almost 11 ½.

"We have been waiting for you. Everyone else is in. You have a little more than a half hour to do ten miles. Can you do it?" the head vet asked me.

"Not if I pull all those ribbons," I said as my heart started to sink. It would have been a fast pace even if I didn't have the pull the ribbons, especially after having already completed forty of the miles.

"It is an easy, fast loop," said one of the competitors who had hung around and was listening. She was an international Endurance competiter who had ridden hundreds of miles all over the world and she urged me on. "Vicki, you and Baby can do it. At least give it a good try! It's a really fast loop."

The manager came over and said, "Forget the rest of the ribbons. Get out there and ride like you stole her!"

"Are you sure? I did agree to pull the ribbons," I said, as I hated to not finish my duty, but at the same time, my spirits lifted at the possibility of completion.

"I would rather see you finish this ride. Now GO!"

"Thank you so much!" I hurriedly said as I hopped on Baby.

We started down the driveway. The few that were still there started yelling. "Go! Go! Go!" even as the vet said. "Go! Go! Go!"

The support at these rides is so heartwarming. "To Finish Is To Win" is the Endurance motto." It fits.

"OK, Baby, let's *go!*" I tapped her with the whip, gave her a nudge with my heels. Away we went. I wasn't sure if we would make it but I would sure give it a royal try.

Across the road was the beginning of the trail. It was a rough woodsy trail and I thought, *I never will get any speed this way.*

I continued anyway and within five minutes we came out to clearing and the side of the road where the "trail" was to be followed. There was a really wonderful shoulder with perfect footing and no hills.

I yelled "Yahoo! Baby!" We started galloping down the side of that road. Although we had been out on trail almost twelve hours, we were invigorated and we got a second wind.

I felt Baby pick up her speed and fly towards the farm she knew was at the end of her radar. For a little horse, she sure could move!

I took a peek at my watch and urged her on more. I wanted so badly to make it on time. Not only for Baby and me but also for the ones who waited for me. Baby had more power and speed than I had known she had and she surprised me when the farm was in site.

Baby whinnied to no one in particular. But it was a bugle of sorts to announce our arrival.

We neared the final corner, the bottom of the driveway of the farm. Baby was blowing heavily from the high speed, pushed on by adrenaline. "Hoah, Baby," I urged going into the turn. She was like a firecracker, and for a brief second, her halter wasn't enough to slow her, as we rollbacked into the driveway..

"This is it," I said, collecting myself for the last straightaway. I looked all the way down the driveway where the finish line was. I saw the timer get up from his chair. Suddenly, the few people waiting were coming out to the driveway with him and began to clap. I wasn't prepared for such a greeting, but it felt good. Baby saw them, too, and although she had galloped so far, she seemed to feel the excitement.

We galloped across the finish line. Pony Power!

"Yeah!"

We made that fifty mile ride in eleven hours, fifty four minutes! Close, but still we made it!

Baby vetted out just fine. She finished with 13 As and 1 B on her score sheet, her best scores yet, even after the final sprint.

The manager had saved me a plate of food, and I went home a very tired but happy rider with Baby, a very tired but hungry pony!

Baby and I had a wonderful year, but it took a lot out of me to ride that long. My body had changed so much after my accident and it was taking a very long time to completely heal.

In 2007, I decided I would retire from competition.

I retired King to a nice retirement home where he would be spoiled rotten. Baby went back to being a school pony with my students. I rode her only for pleasure.

JUST SOMETHING ABOUT HER!

I felt my husband and I needed a change. We wanted to spend more time visiting our children and grandchildren who lived in other states. It was very hard to travel when we had animals.

In the past, I would pay someone to "house, horse, and dog" sit. It was expensive and always something happened while we were away that made us worry the whole time instead of enjoying our trip. I wasn't quite ready to let go of the horses just then, but it had been in the back of my mind for about a year. I wasn't having as much fun riding as I used to. My usual companions were also riding less and less. I had given up competition because it hurt to ride that long. I needed to work because we were trying to remodel the house and landscape our yard. There became less time and money for horses.

So in the fall of 2010 I decided to find homes for Baby and the remaining horses.

Baby, although a great school horse, had a little bit of an attitude if not handled correctly. Even though she was older now, she still could be very witchy.

I made a couple calls to riding schools I thought she would fit in with. I thought of the Therapeutic Riding School where Boy had gone to for the remainder of his life, but didn't want Baby that far from me.

I chose to place Baby at Painted Pony Sport Horses and Equestrian Center, which is owned and run by Pat and Cassie Martin. It was my intention that Baby would work with people of all ages and abilities, much as she had done most of her life.

"Hey, Baby Girl, how are you doing?" Baby nickered as I walked to the stall. It had only been a day but I had to see her.

Pat saw me drive in from the house. She came out, walked over and asked, "She is doing OK, but is she always this quiet?"

"Well, she is a fairly laid back pony but she doesn't really look right." I remarked to Pat. "What's the matter, Baby Girl?" I petted her, gave her a treat and looked into her eyes. They were sad eyes and made my heart sink. She should love it here.

"I think it will just take her time to get used to the new routine," said Pat.

I could see she was a little worried about Baby.

I replied, "She has never had a problem with going anywhere. I have taken her away from home a lot in the past. Can't imagine she wouldn't be OK."

Baby *didn't* do so well. She became depressed. I visited her daily for the first week and watched as she got quieter and quieter. I could see that she wasn't happy but couldn't figure out why. She had a nice stall (that she didn't seem to want to leave at first), and had plenty of attention. In a paddock by herself, she seemed OK, but she didn't seem to care and acted just a little too quiet. This wasn't Baby.

Thinking she needed and was ready for company, Pat put her out with one of the other horses her size. She promptly chased it out through the fence. That didn't work!

Since I had mentioned how aggressive she was towards other horses in the pasture, she was put in a pasture with three ponies Pat called the *mean* ponies. Pat thought she would fit in. Those ponies chased *her*

across the brook and wouldn't let her come back across, not even to eat. So once the grass was gone over there, she went hungry.

"Seriously?" I asked when I saw Pat next. "*They* chased *her*? Didn't she fight back?"

"No, and by the time I realized they were not letting her eat, she had lost weight. I went out to get her and she dragged me out the gate. I just don't know where she will fit in!" Pat replied. "I am really worried about her," she continued.

I waited a week or so to visit again, thinking maybe I was visiting too often. I also wanted to let them figure it out. I wanted her to get used to their routine. So once again she lived in the stall for a while and was put out by herself.

On the next visit, I realized that she not only looked sad and depressed but also had lost considerable weight, something very hard for a pony to do, especially Piggy Baby!

Pat's daughter, Cassie, was getting ready to train a horse and was in the barn, so I mentioned it. I started asking all kinds of questions about her care and how she was acting. I could see that she had plenty of hay in her stall, but she was not eating! And that was a new thing for me to see.

I realized that I had insulted them when Cassie snapped at me, "You are welcome to move her if you want."

The hurt look in her eye was something I didn't intend to inflict and certainly didn't want to see. They were doing everything possible to make Baby comfortable. I knew that, but just wanted to see if I could figure it out with them.

My first thought, as my heart was breaking because of Baby's condition was, *you bet I want to move her—right back home!*

Immediately, my second thought was, *if I take her home now, not only would she be alone but that would defeat my whole purpose for placing her in the first place.* These thoughts happened with lightning speed.

Again I could see that I had insulted a friend, but Baby is such a part of me. I don't think I really realized it until then.

I knew I had to apologize as I didn't mean they didn't take good care, I was only concerned that she was so thin in such a short time. I was hurting to see her like that. I was very surprised that she wasn't happy with so many horses for friends and with so much activity to keep her entertained.

"I am sorry Cassie. I didn't mean you were not taking care of her. It just hurts me to see her like that. She is usually such a scrapper. Such a happy pony. I really thought she would love it here."

Cassie accepted my apology. We talked about it for a minute or two. Cassie had to work the horse she had ready and standing in the cross ties, so I let her go.

I visited Baby for a little while. Groomed her and fed her goodies. I then went home, with a very heavy heart and anxiety that I hadn't felt in a very long time. It made me think of the last time I had let her go to another home and how I could see her just not right.

That night Pat called me. "I am really worried about Baby," she began. "I think she misses *you*! I don't know what to do with her. She doesn't seem to get along with anyone. Either she chases them off or they chase her off. What do you want to do?"

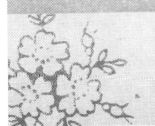

I told her about my visit and how bad I felt that I had hurt Cassie's feelings and that I had apologized. I also apologized to Pat.

We talked about Baby a while longer. They really wanted it to work. I said I would give it another month before moving her.

"Do you mind if I come over and take her out for a little ride and do some hands on healing?" I asked.

"No, come and do whatever you want to. You are always welcome here."

"OK, I will be there tomorrow after work," I said.

"Hi, Baby Girl. Want to go for a ride?" I asked as I walked to her paddock. She nickered and trotted over to me. This was the most animated I had seen her since taking her there.

I groomed her. I talked to her. I got out the bareback pad and put that on along with her hackamore. I then took her over to the mounting block, hopped on, rode out the driveway and up the road.

I only rode perhaps two miles just her and me in a calm quiet ride. We mostly walked, but I trotted and cantered just a bit to feel how she was moving. I talked to her and sang a little bit. I had meditated earlier so I could be in a peaceful frame of mind.

"That was like old times, huh, Baby?" I said as I dismounted. I took off her bareback pad, groomed her again, and picked out her feet. I kissed her nose and gave her some Apple Wafers.

I took three really deep calming breaths. "OK, Baby, lets see if we can make you feel better." I began by placing my right hand on her pole, my left on her brow. Barely touching Baby with butterfly like pressure, I took another deep breath, closed my eyes and thought. *Baby, everything is going to be all right. You will like it here if you give yourself a chance.*

Baby lowered her head. I opened my eyes a little but stayed quiet.

With her eyes at half mast, her lower lip twitching and beginning to hang, I could feel her truly starting to relax. She heaved a huge sigh, swaying a little. She began to chew. A drop of drool developed in the corner of her mouth, and slowly dripped to the floor.

I then ran my left hand along and down her neck, stopping where the shoulder and neck meet. I ran my right hand across the top of her crest, over her withers and stopped just behind the withers. Again with butterfly pressure, I took a deep breath and thought of general physical healing. I stood like this for perhaps twenty minutes. I could feel a lot of heat releasing from Baby's body and a tingle in my hands. Baby began to yawn over and over again as her eyes completely closed. Her ears were flopped to the side, relaxed, and she was softly chewing and continuing her yawning.

I felt better. I thought Baby felt better. I took my hands and stroked her from head to tail and down her legs in long soothing strokes.

"Baby, I hope that makes you believe that I have not abandoned you. I will visit you often. I will bring the grandchildren to ride you. You will be OK. I just know you will."

I gave her some more treats. Then put her back into the paddock. She looked peaceful when I left. With one hind leg resting on the toe, head and neck level with her withers, she was completely relaxed.

Pat called me that very night. "I don't know what you did, but Baby is a totally different horse tonight! I put her out with two quiet Warmbloods and she is doing great! She is eating and they are not bothering her and she is not bothering them. That is such a dramatic difference."

I recanted what my afternoon with Baby was like.

They had put her out with two horses that were kind but so big that Pat didn't think Baby would push them around. Baby seemed to get along with them in a passive way, neither fighting nor being pushed around, simply being in with *the girls*. She was very happy with her new pasture mates. She was even mutually grooming with them by the end of the week.

Phew! I thought. *She was going to be alright.*

I held off from visiting trying to let her find her own way.

Then came the day I once again visited her. She saw me and called to me from across the ring. Her paddock being on the other side, I was very surprised she could recognize me so far away.

"Hey, Baby Girl!" I called to her. I went into the barn to get her halter and an Apple Wafer. She was right at the gate, nickering to me by the time I got there. Her eyes still looked sad but so much better, not depressed or scared like before. I still had that feeling of loss, but felt that she was finally OK and would be happy soon.

She had gained her weight back so I knew she was eating just fine.

When I had placed Baby with Pat and Cassie, I had filled them in on Baby's foundering. Now to see her *not* eating with a round bale available all day was amazing to me. I guessed that because she knew it was there when she wanted it, she didn't feel the need to eat all the time.

She seemed fine, and Cassie was able to use her for lessons. There was one little girl that really liked Baby and wanted to ride her every lesson.

I stayed away, visiting about once a week. For some reason I was still worried about her, and I wasn't sleeping well at all. *Why did I feel this way?*

I drove by Pat and Cassie's farm during my daily commute to work. I could see Baby in her paddock, that she was fine with her new friends, but it took all I could muster not to stop and see her every single day.

Almost two months after I placed Baby there, I realized just how much I missed her in my life! Not just riding, but just simply being near her. I had had her for most of her twenty one years and wasn't ready to simply forget her and move on with my life.

Not knowing quite what to do, I called Pat to ask if I could come and talk with her. I could tell by her voice that she was suspicious of my call. I almost chickened out as I was sure she would be very upset at me for even suggesting taking Baby back when she had just settled in.

I arrived and started to explain that I had made a mistake and wanted to have her back. We had made an agreement at the beginning that if it didn't work out or either of us wanted to change the situation we could as no money had exchanged hands.

"Pat, I really miss Baby." I started sobbing almost before the words could come out of my mouth.

I could see the shock on Pat's face at my burst of tears. She walked over and gave me a huge hug and said, "Do you want to take her back? You can have her back. I thought of her as yours anyway." She understood completely, adding, "I couldn't believe you could just simply give her away anyway. You have had Baby most of her life!"

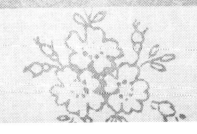

I felt relief, and with it came more tears that seemed to cleanse me. Pat was right. I simply couldn't give her away. Baby was my partner and companion.

Baby is her old self again. She is peppy and young acting. I've continued boarding Baby with Pat and Cassie. Not only is Baby happy there, but it I can still have freedom to come and go as I please.

I visit Baby daily. If I don't ride, I groom, massage, do healing, or simply let her graze. We enjoy ourselves on the trails, conditioning for Limited Distance rides, and take lessons from Cassie.

We are finding new adventures. Just Baby and me. Together. A new chapter in our lives.

Who knows what the future will bring.

Baby and Vicki 2011

FAMILY --- FRIENDS --- STUDENTS

Baby

By M. (age 5)

Baby is a cute horsey. She is the best horse that I could ever ride. I love Baby. She is really smart.

M. riding in the woods. Summer of 2011

Baby

By C. (age 13)

I have known Baby all my life. I rode her before I could even ride a bike. She is amazingly smart and that is one feature that makes her wonderful with young riders.

One of the features that makes her wonderful with kids is that she is calm and does not get spooked easily. She is also slightly smaller which makes her easier to ride. As I said before she is very smart so she knows exactly what to do. All of these features makes her easy for kids to ride.

Not only is she good with kids but she is also very fun for experienced riders like my Nana and beginner to intermediate riders like me. Baby is very calm but can give a good gallop when you want her to. She is a very well rounded horse.

Even though she is getting older that doesn't seem to affect anything about her. She rides very well and is just as good as ever. Baby has been many places and through many adventures.

Baby is a horse I will always remember...and love.

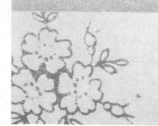

C. riding in field. Summer Of 2011

Baby

I have fun riding her. And to me it's fun and amazing. So we need to ride

more. I like to do the exercises most of all. I like to ride when it is hot in the Summer. I like to ride in the

woods. I ride her a lot. Seems to me I have been riding for a very long time. I can't wait to ride again. I wish

Baby lived at Nana's so I could see her every day.   Love CD. Age 10

doing exersices

Baby

By Mae Kolln (age 11)

When I first started riding Baby I started out in the ring and I didn't know how to ride. But once I started riding in the woods things were easier.

Baby made it easier cause she's a pony and not an incredibly tall horse. Sometimes she would have a temper but she only bit me once, because I wasn't being cautious. And she doesn't like being saddled up. But she helps you when you're putting the bridle on her. Other than that she's fun to ride.

When we start out for a ride she walks very slow. But whenever we're on our way back she walks at medium speed because the barn's her home and that's where the food is. If it's been a while since the last time I rode her, she'd be full of energy. When we start cantering she'd start to buck because she's loving the chance to finally have some space to run. But I never fell off of her once when she bucked. The 2 times I fell off was the time I was riding her bareback and I didn't see the tree in front of me, so the tree pushed me off of her. Another time I fell off of her was when we were doing emergency evacuation from the horse I kind of messed up and had a rough landing. The thing is about Baby, whenever you fall off, she won't keep going, she'll just stop.

Once I got older it got easier to ride her. Before, she would stop at every bush she came to and start eating. So I would have to pull her head up. But like I said, once I got older, it was smooth sailing from there. That's the end of my adventure.

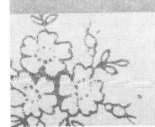

Baby

By K. (age 20)

I just remember jumping with her. And at the end of the lesson I fell off, and both Vicki and Abby encouraged me to get back on Baby, and that for both of our sakes needed to end the lesson on a good note. So I got back on her, and we did it! And to be completely honest, jumping ended up being my favorite thing to do with a horse ---

BABY

by Karma (age 10)

She is gentle and loving. She is always there for you. She is beautiful, brave and smart. When she left my site I would cry and cry. If I could see her one more time I would no longer cry and cry. I would be so excited.

I had so much fun with her. I remember one time I would ride her and I refused to go up a huge hill.

I also remember when I would ride her on a trail. A board was in my way, Mom threw the board and the bang startled her. She jumped up on two legs and I almost fell off. I'll always remember that. P.S. Love Ya.

BABY

by Karma (age 10)

I wasn't going up the hill

I wasn't doing any sort of thing.

Just because I was scared.

But when they made me go up

It wasn't all so bad

All because of Baby

The Crooked River 30

By Abigail Austin

Written October 27, 1998 (Age 15)

I had no reason to be nervous, but I was. Huge butterflies were racing around in my stomach, and my heart rate was most likely in the thousands. I went over to the paddock gate to say hi to the little, spotted mare, who was trying to get to the green grass on the other side of the fence. Baby was always eating. I often called her Piglet. World War III could be going on right around her, but she'd never notice if food was available. I wished I could have been as calm as Baby was at that moment. As the mare approached me with a gentle nicker, I calmed slightly.

My riding instructor, Vicki, came up beside me. "Take a deep breath and relax, Abby," she said. Her voice always sounded calm and collected. "You're going to do great."

Together we put my gear into the back of the truck and loaded Baby into the trailer. Boy and Banner, the two remaining horses at the stable, hollered to Baby as we drove away. She was the third horse to leave the stable that day to go to the ride. The two other horses belonged to Vicki and her husband, Ron. King, Vicki's horse, was a gray Arabian, and Sierra, Ron's, was a pinto Spanish Mustang. Both have done many Competitive Trail and Endurance rides much like the one that we'd all be going on the next morning. Vicki and King were pros at it having completed many lengthy rides. Ron and Sierra were making their way up there. Baby and I, on the other hand, were rookies at this, and I had no idea what to expect.

When we pulled into the Waterford Fair Grounds in the hills of Western Maine, I was amazed at all of the horses. My heart was pounding so hard, I was afraid it may pop out of my chest, but a big a grin came over me anyway. I could hardly believe this weekend had finally come! Baby and I had been conditioning for this ride all summer. I hoped that hard work would pay off.

The first thing to do was the initial vet check. In Competitive Trail Riding, the judges are veterinarians. Winners of the competition are determined by the condition of the rider's horse at the end of the ride compared to the beginning. The vets looked Baby over for any marks that she may have so that they may not be mistaken for new marks at the end of the ride. Then I trotted Baby in hand. During this portion of the check, the vets are looking for pre-existing lameness and Baby's gait. This was also the best way to see a horse's "before energy" in order to gage fatigue. Here was where I would lose points.

Baby was anxious. She was almost uncontrollable. I had separated her from her herd. King and Sierra whinnied to her from the barn, and she screeched and snorted back to them. She bucked and cantered rather than trotted. I bet that blade of grass she'd been reaching for through the fence at the stable wouldn't have distracted her then. The vets described Baby as "feisty," which wasn't her normal. Baby's normal when we practiced our trot outs at home was easy. In fact, I carried a crop to urge her forward. I had it with me during the real check, but I didn't need it. In strange places, horses often felt more attached than usual to horses they know, and when Baby was back with King and Sierra after the vet check, she was her calm, normal self, concerned only with munching hay.

With Baby settled, it was time to set up camp. I unpacked our supplies, checked over her tack, and set up my tent. I went to bed wide awake from anticipation of the day ahead. Baby and I had ridden on numerous trail rides, but this was my first trail competition. It wouldn't be just any ride. Eventually, I relaxed into sleep. After all, 5:30 a.m. would come bright and early.

Actually we were up before the sun. While Baby gobbled down her grain and hay, I had a granola bar and hot apple cider, which felt wonderful on my throat and chilled hands. It was forty degrees that October morning. A short hour after breakfast, it was time to mount.

If I thought the butterflies in my stomach the day before were huge, the one I had then was the size of Godzilla's friend, Mothra. Baby, too, was just as anxious, especially when she realized King and Sierra had started on the ride without her. Two riders left at a time in two-minute intervals. Time was important. There was a specific amount of time to complete the ride. One minute too early or too late in that time window, and competitors would be penalized. Vicki and Ron were numbers three and four, which meant I would leave two minutes later in the next pair. Those two minutes I waited to leave felt more like two hours!

I was a wreck, and so was Baby. We just added tension to one another. Baby felt upset that her barn mates had left, and she tugged on my reins and bounced in place as she tried to follow. I understood her feeling. I would have done anything to be riding behind Vicki at that moment. In the same way King and Sierra's presence kept Baby calm, my teacher could assure me.

Finally, number five—that's us!—and off I started on the 1998 Crooked River 30. The next 30 miles were amazing (at least once my apprehension alleviated)!

For the first five miles, Baby and I were very uptight. As cold as it was, Baby had broken out a sweat. Eventually, we found our pace behind the horse and rider we started with. That was when we realized that this was just another trail ride like the ones we did at home conditioning for this big day.

"We can do this, Baby Girl," I said quietly.

Baby flicked her ears backward, listening to my words, and she lowered her head. She was the first horse I rode when I started taking riding lessons with Vicki. As nervous as I was mounting her, she calmly stood, eventually taking slow, careful steps, urging me that it was OK, and I trusted her. Now during our training, she trusted me when I urged her forward, even if a dog threatened or a logging truck hogged the road or if thunder rattled the sky. If I told her it was OK, she believed me. Although Baby belonged to Vicki, she and I were partners, and we connected. Yes, our nerves snowballed from that connection, but they also dissipated as we began to rely on each other and gain our independence. Here was a team in action.

The terrain consisted of back roads and trails through woods and pasture. Some parts had lots of loose rock and roots; others were muddy, a perfect place for horses to lose shoes. I was glad Baby was sure-footed. I would release a simple long breath and sit deep in the saddle, and she would calmly, gently make her way through the obstacles.

Eventually, we caught up with Vicki and Ron. Immediately, Baby and I let go any leftover tension. When I saw Vicki, she was smiling brightly. She looked proud, and that gave me confidence.

Time sure flew! Fifteen miles felt like five, but I knew we were half-way because we were riding into the hold. This was our half hour (mandatory time) to break and go through the midway vet check. The vets looked over each horse and read metabolic signs. They were tracking lameness, hydration, fatigue, and anything that could prevent a horse from continuing. Baby didn't act feisty this time. She was her normal self; she even pulled me toward the green grass on the side of the track during our trot out.

Following the check, it was break time. Horses came first, as Vicki taught me, and I made sure Baby had food, water, and comfort. Once her needs were met, I had my chance to do the same before we started again.

But this time, Baby and I were relaxed. There were no butterflies as we waited for our turn to leave. As we started off behind Vicki and Ron, I smiled. Yup, piece of cake.

The whole ride was a pretty steady pace, most of the time a trot. Baby, whose legs were shorter than King's and Sierra's, kept up by regularly sneaking into a canter. I loved her canter that day. It was smooth and forward. It felt as if we were moving together, a connection we hadn't yet made during our Dressage lessons. This was part of our partnership. One time, Baby broke into a gallop. The most exciting feeling I've ever experienced is riding a galloping horse.

Finally the finish line was within sight, and a wave of triumph came over me. I trotted Baby up beside King, and Vicki smiled down at me. She had been across these finish lines many times, even in the weary hours of the night having ridden one hundred miles in twenty hours. I loved today's competition. I was excited to compete again. Maybe someday, it would be me up there, like my teacher, crossing the finish line of a famous race.

"Yee ha!" I shouted as we crossed the line.

But crossing the finish line didn't mean the end of the event in Competitive Trail Riding. Besides the horses needing care after carrying their riders many miles, there was the final visit to the vets— one last hands on check, one last metabolic read, and one last trot out.

Although I could have ridden all day, it felt good to finish...and to get off! I was used to riding long distances, but thirty was the farthest I had been on horseback, and I was tired. Baby was, as well. In the barn, after I had un-tacked her, she could have fallen asleep while I rubbed her down.

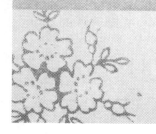

In the next hour, the vets examined Baby, checking her pulse and respiration, and I trotted her out again for them to see if she was lame. She seemed great—in fact, had she not felt herd bound during her first trot out, I think there would have been minimal change in Baby's condition. That meant our conditioning was a success.

When that was over, and Baby was put in her stall with an afternoon snack, it was my turn for a break. I got dinner, took a seat and began gobbling. Mothra had flown away, and now my stomach was ready for food. I cleaned my plate easily, and stuck the apple in my pocket for later for Baby.

Soon after the riders were fed and everyone's scores were tallied, it was time for awards. Being a rookie at this, I didn't expect Baby and me to do outstanding. All that mattered was that we finished and had fun doing it. Check for both. The first awards were given to the junior division. When my name was called to come up and get my ribbons and score sheets, I was very excited, but I didn't realize immediately my placing. Vicki whispered in my ear as I sat back down. My eyes bulged out and my jaw dropped open when it clicked.

Baby and I had gotten first place! A blue ribbon! I was the top junior rider!

Sure there were only a few riders, but we got a great score, 94%, which was very good for my first time. I was called up a second time for top rookie. Now I had three ribbons: Maroon for completion, green for top junior, and the ribbon I was most proud, a blue! I was so happy and couldn't wait to see Baby.

Up at the barn after the awards, I threw my arms around her neck, giving her a big hug. I was so proud of her efforts that day, and how well she and I both did. We were a great team! We worked hard for our goal, and we succeeded.

Vicki came up beside us. She patted Baby on her neck and put her other arm around me. "Great job, Abby!"

"I had so much fun, Vicki!" I said, hugging her back. "Thank you!"

Baby shoved her spotted nose in between us, nickering excitedly, wanting to be included in the hug. Then she crunched her teeth through my pocket, finding the apple. To Baby, a red apple was better than a blue ribbon.

This horse had given me confidence, partnership, and an amazing ride, and for this she'd forever be in my heart. I rubbed her forehead and giggled with her happy nickers as she enjoyed her apple.

Abby and Baby following King and Vicki
on Crooked River 30

Baby

by Aimee McKeen(age 21)

The day I met Baby I was in the second grade. My grandmother had given me a gift of riding lessons for my birthday, and I had spent the entire previous night thinking of all the exciting things I would do in my first lesson. I pictured a huge white horse that I would gallop around the ring, and I might even be able to do some jumps!

When I arrived at the barn I met Vicki. She was chatty and welcoming, and we talked about horses and school and how much fun we would have. She walked me into the barn, and before me was no white stallion. It was a sassy little appaloosa, named Baby.

I took the first few minutes petting and brushing her. Baby was just as interested in me as I was in her, and she smelled me and watched me the entire time. Vicki showed me how to groom her, and then how to put her saddle on. I was really nervous when it finally came to actually ride, and as Vicki helped me on Baby all the crazy jumps that I'd been thinking about the night before left my mind, and I concentrated on just keeping my balance. Our first little path around the ring was spent just getting comfortable with each other. In those first awkward moments I had no idea how much time we would spend together, how we would get to know each other, and what a great team we would make.

I spent most of my child hood exploring the woods of Maine with Baby, bee bopping along behind Vicki and King. Baby was just as headstrong as I was, and we kept right up with the adults and the "big" horses. We learned the basics in the ring, but it was the long rides through the forest that we really loved. When we

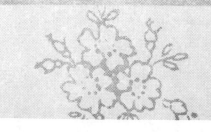

first started riding together it was short rides through the Cornwall Nature Preserve, but the longer we rode together the further we would go. I remember how much fun we would have just galloping down a dirt road, my awkward first trip through a brook (I almost took a bath!), and bouncing around through snowdrifts that were nearly as tall as we were!

One day as Baby and I were galloping along she took a sharp turn and my saddle wasn't tight enough. Before I knew it my saddle was on her belly and I was on the ground. I wasn't hurt, but the spill scared me quite a bit. I stood up, crying a little. Baby, who after a second, realized I wasn't on her back ran back to me. Vicki and King rode up, and Vicki said I had to get back on. Now, I'd always heard the saying "If you fall out of the saddle you have to get right back on", but I'd never realized how scary it looked until now. I don't actually remember how long it took me to get back on, but I know Vicki had to jump off King and basically force me into the saddle. I still remember how scared I was, and how slow and easy Baby moved until I started to relax. Sometimes even now, when I get something messed up or I get nervous I remember how proud I was by the time we got back to the barn that I had gotten back into the saddle.

One day Vicki asked me if I would like to ride Baby in a 50 mile endurance ride. I was so excited and so nervous! We had never ridden that far before but we were ready for it! My grandmother brought her camper for us to stay in the night before the ride, and I was so excited I could barely sleep. We woke up early the next morning and got ready. The truth is the miles flew by! We had so much fun- not only riding all over Buckfield Maine, but also getting to see other riders and horses as well. After all the riding we had done Baby was in excellent shape, and she did amazing during the ride! We crossed the finish line two happy campers (And the winners of our age group!).

Even now, over ten years later I still remember all the happy memories I had with Baby. We trusted each other (I can't imagine doing around the world on another horse!), she always knew how to make me feel better if I was having an off day, and I loved her competitive spirit. She always gave her best and had such a sassy personality. I'm so lucky to have had so many amazing times with her, and I'm sure she's still the sassy little appaloosa that I met so long ago. Just thinking of all the fun we had together makes me smile. Like Winston Churchill said, "There is something about the outside of a horse that is good for the inside of a man".

Baby and Aimee

Abby and Baby

Abby and BAby geting
vetted at hold.

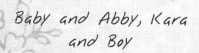

Abby on Baby, Kara
on Boy in Christmas
Parade

Baby and Abby, Kara
and Boy

Baby and
vicki 2011.

Baby Face June 8th 2011

Baby in good form
June 8th 2011

enjoying a ride
on BAby

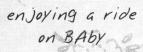

first ride!

fooling around

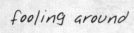

Hello!

Love!

164

mom and child ready
for a trail ride.

mom and child
trail ride

ready to ride winter
of 2011

riding by herself for the first time!

training a young horse

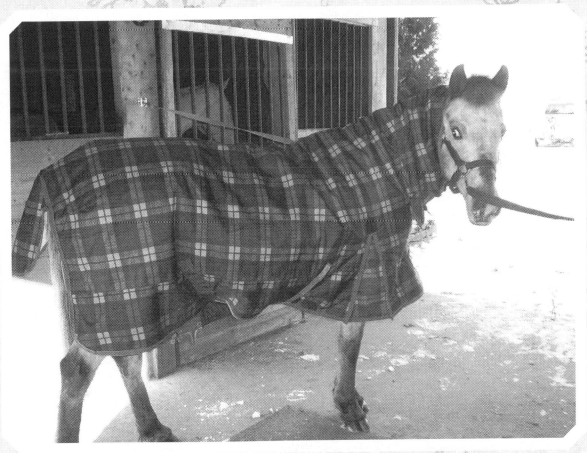

Winter 2010 2011 Baby ready for that snow